MONUMENTS

MONUMENTS

Stones That Help

RALPH D. CURTIN

RESOURCE *Publications* • Eugene, Oregon

MONUMENTS
Stones That Help

Copyright © 2020 Ralph D. Curtin. All rights reserved. Except for brief quotations in critical publications or reviews, no part of this book may be reproduced in any manner without prior written permission from the publisher. Write: Permissions, Wipf and Stock Publishers, 199 W. 8th Ave., Suite 3, Eugene, OR 97401.

Resource Publications
An Imprint of Wipf and Stock Publishers
199 W. 8th Ave., Suite 3
Eugene, OR 97401

www.wipfandstock.com

PAPERBACK ISBN: 978-1-7252-6854-8
HARDCOVER ISBN: 978-1-7252-6855-5
EBOOK ISBN: 978-1-7252-6856-2

Manufactured in the U.S.A.   03/25/20

"These stones are to be a memorial
to the people of Israel forever. . ."

Joshua 4:7

Contents

Preface | ix
Chapter One: Monuments: Good And Bad | 1
Chapter Two: Ancient World Monuments | 6
Chapter Three: America's Monuments | 11
Chapter Four: God's Monuments | 22
Chapter Five: Monuments To Israel's Preservation | 37
Chapter Six: Monuments To Sin And Conflict | 46
Chapter Seven: Personal Victory Monuments | 60
Chapter Eight: Recognizing Your Monuments | 68
Chapter Nine: The Ultimate Crowning Glory Monument | 78
Appendix A: Prayer of National Repentance | 81
Bibliography | 83

Preface

Since the beginning of time, both God and man have left monuments to their existence, their history, their purpose, their laws, their achievements and failures, and their testimonies. These memorials are etched on stones, written on papyrus, parchments, and animal skins, and in modern times, recorded on computer hard drives. They represent *stones that help us*. The stones help us remember the past, both good and bad, and to instruct us on how to conduct our lives in the future.

From a Biblical perspective, God told Moses to record His name and that the Name of God, I AM, was to be remembered from generation to generation (Exodus 3:15 KJV). Thus, the name of God was to be a memorial to His wonderful works to mankind for all eternity. The writing of God's Law on stone tablets represented the divine will of God defining the proper relationship between God and man and man toward his fellow man. Later to Joshua, the God of Israel instructed him to erect a monument of stones to commemorate the miraculous crossing through the Jordan to the Promise Land (Joshua 4:1–9 KJV). In Psalms, God reminded the faithful that His Name endured forever and was to be praised and remembered above the name of any and all idols (Psalm 135:13–21). In First Samuel, Samuel commemorates the Israelites victory over the Philistines at Eben-ezer and to memorialize the event, he took a stone and set it up and called the name of it *Eben-ezer* saying, "Hitherto has the LORD helped us" (7:12). The stone represented a monument to Israel's past victory that would be a helpful reminder of God's deliverance of future battles. It was a stone that helped them remember.

Preface

Mankind together with God's Spirit have kept a record of these memorials in the Bible that have become landmarks that lead to God for others to follow and bring Him glory and honor.

From a human perspective, mankind has left an indelible record throughout the ages of his existence and achievements. Pillars, megaliths, statues, along with written tributes, and magnetic recordings of historical and archeological importance continue to grace our world to serve as reminders of good and bad events; special and not-so-special places, and of man's accomplishments and, unfortunately, his misdeeds as well. In all to many cases, these misdeeds have become landmarks that have caused many to turn away from God and they in turn have recruited others to follow them down a path to shame and ignominy that have become an international disgrace.

Monuments [Lt. *monere*, meaning "to remind," or "to advise" or "to warn"] come in many forms. There are statues, buildings, and other structures erected to commemorate an important architectural heritage or a famous or notable person or event that may include historical evidences worth remembering throughout the ages. Burial places, cenotaphs, obelisks, crosses, tombs, tombstones, grave markers, mausoleums and shrines provide reminders of significant deceased persons or memorable battlegrounds.

America's Drive-In theaters, Disney World, Coney Island, and many other amusement parks in the United States remain to this day to be monuments to family fun, entertainment, and happy times. God, too, has left, and continues to leave monuments to his goodness and mercy and He has left it for us to discover and realize its purpose—to bring us closer to Himself. They are *stones that help us.*

CHAPTER ONE

Monuments: Good And Bad

Why do you think monuments are a good idea? How can they help me in times of discouragement?

First, what is a monument or stone? I remember they had a phase of owning "pet rocks." Is it something like that? Much more; they are a physical reminder of a specific date and time when God intervened in my life and brought me through a crisis to His glory and honor.

Did you ever pray for something for a long period of time and despair of an answer? Then all of a sudden, possibly the last 30 minutes, the prayer was answered. Acknowledge God's intervention and record it on a rock or stone for future edification. God was faithful then, why should I doubt Him now?

Right now I have a large tray where I keep my recorded stones as monuments to my Faithful and True God. When I take the time to pick each one up and read the inscription, I am humbled by the goodness of the Lord in my life and I am encouraged to praise Him for His divine care.

As you read this first chapter you will be reminded of our sovereign God who intervenes in the lives of men and nations.

Monuments

Monuments, representing both good and evil, are scattered around our planet as mute memorials to humanity's treatment of their fellow man.

Who can forget the United States Marine Corps iconic image of the six servicemen who raised the second U.S. flag on Mount Suribachi during the Battle of Iwo Jima during World War II on February 23, 1945? Associated Press photographer Joe Rosenthal achieved instant fame when his photo was released showing the American victory over the Japanese-entrenched island. It is a memorial that stands today, emblematic of the valor of the fighting men who risked their lives for freedom. It is a representation of the indomitable spirit of those who defend America against tyranny.

On April 22, 1945, four days after Nuremberg, Germany fell, the US Army blew up the gold-plated and laurel-wreathed swastika—the symbol of the Nazi regime that was to stand for thousands of years. The monument placed atop the Zeppelin Grandstand, constructed under the management of Albert Speer to memorialize Adolph Hitler's Party Rally Grounds was to emulate the great cathedrals of antiquity. Nothing remains of the monument to evil today.

On April 9, 2003, the Internet and world news networks ran live video footage of the toppling of Saddam Hussein's 39-foot high statue in Firdos Square in Bagdad shortly after the Iraq War invasion. The destruction of the figure marked the symbolic end of the Battle of Baghdad. Once toppled, the Iraqi citizens decapitated the statue and dragged it through the streets of the city hitting it with their shoes—symbolizing the fall of the Hussein government. Nothing remains of the statue to an evil regime today.

In 2014, the Islamic State (ISIS) took control of Mosul in Iraq and began a campaign to destroy historic mosques and shrines that were memorials to local Sunni Muslims that challenged ISIS's radical interpretation of Islam. Using sledgehammers, the radical ISIS jihadists' targeted sites dedicated to popular religious figures such as the tomb of Jonah the prophet, most famous for surviving being swallowed by a whale in the Biblical narrative.

In March of 2015, ISIS was charged by the United Nations with war crimes for the bulldozing of the ancient city of Nimrud. ISIS is engaging in the systematic campaign to decimate Iraq's rich heritage that dates back to the 13th century B.C.E. considered to be the jewel of the Assyrian era. Experts claimed the ISIS movement justified the destructions by saying the statues are idolatrous but other experts say the jihadists traffic antiquities to fund their self-proclaimed "caliphate" and only destroy the pieces that are too bulky to be smuggled.

Why would they do such a thing? Because they wanted to wipe out another culture's legacy so they could create their own. Throughout the ages, every society or radical movement wants a permanent legacy that will survive even the destructive efforts of warmongers. Time and history will record the monuments to misery and death of these Satanic-inspired destroyers.

In stark contrast, the Cross of Christ stands today as an enduring monument to the salvation of the Lord, eclipsing all other monuments as a God-given memorial to His grace and love for all of His creation. No other monument has that message to the world.

Since the beginning of time, both God and man have left monuments to their existence, their history, their purpose, their laws, their achievements and failures, and their testimonies. These memorials are etched on stones, written on papyrus, parchments, and animal skins, and in modern times, recorded on computer hard drives. They represent stones that help us. The stones help us remember the past, both good and bad, and to instruct us on how to conduct our lives in the future.

From a Biblical perspective, God told Moses to record His name and that the Name of God, I AM, was to be remembered from generation to generation (Exodus 3:15 KJV). Thus, the name of God was to be a memorial to His wonderful works to mankind for all eternity. The writing of God's Law on stone tablets represented the divine will of God defining the proper relationship between God and man and man toward his fellow man. Later to Joshua, the God of Israel instructed him to erect a monument of stones to commemorate the miraculous crossing through the Jordan to the Promise Land (Joshua 4:1-9 KJV). In Psalms, God reminded the faithful that His Name endured forever and was to be praised and remembered above the name of any and all idols (Psalm 135:13–21). In 1 Samuel, Samuel commemorates the Israelites victory over the Philistines at Eben-ezer and to memorialize the event, he took a stone and set it up and called the name of it Eben-ezer saying, "Hitherto has the LORD helped us" (7:12). The stone represented a monument to Israel's past victory that would be a helpful reminder of God's deliverance of future battles. It was a stone that helped them remember.

We will explore in the following chapters the importance of having stones that help you remember events you may have overlooked as you travel through life that are indeed a blessing to you.

Mankind together with God's Spirit have kept a record of these memorials in the Bible that have become landmarks that lead to God for others to follow and bring Him glory and honor.

From a human perspective, mankind has left an indelible record throughout the ages of his existence and achievements. Pillars, megaliths, statues, along with written tributes, and magnetic recordings of historical and archeological importance continue to grace our world to serve as reminders of good and bad events; special and not-so-special places, and of man's accomplishments and, unfortunately, his misdeeds as well. In all to many cases, these misdeeds have become landmarks that have caused many to turn away from God and they in turn have recruited others to follow them down a path to shame and ignominy that have become an international disgrace.

Monuments [Lt. monere, meaning "to remind," or "to advise" or "to warn"] come in many forms. There are statues, buildings, and other structures erected to commemorate an important architectural heritage or a famous or notable person or event that may include historical evidences worth remembering throughout the ages. Burial places, cenotaphs, obelisks, crosses, tombs, tombstones, grave markers, mausoleums and shrines provide reminders of significant deceased persons or memorable battlegrounds.

Monuments: Good And Bad

America's Drive-In theaters, Disney World, Coney Island, and many other amusement parks in the United States remain to this day to be monuments to family fun, entertainment, and happy times. God, too, has left, and continues to leave monuments to his goodness and mercy and He has left it for us to discover and realize its purpose—to bring us closer to Himself. They are stones that help us.

CHAPTER TWO

Ancient World Monuments

THE PYRAMID OF CHEOPS

For thousands of years man has stood in awe at the magnificent monuments that have been left behind as tributes to ancient civilizations and kingdoms. One such stone memorial is the Pyramid of Khufu or the Pyramid of Cheops located in the desert of El Giza, Egypt. This great burial tomb built for the fourth dynasty Egyptian Pharaoh Khufu consists of an estimated 2.3 million blocks of limestone that required a workforce of at least 14,567 people and a peak workforce of 40,000 people working for 20 years. Built with high precision, this monument was the tallest man-made structure in the world for over 3,800 years and is the oldest of the Seven Wonders of the Ancient World, and the only one to remain somewhat intact. This great extant architectural masterpiece of the ancient world is a testimonial to man's ability to preserve and record their presence and existence. In many ways the Pyramid of Cheops represents past accomplishments by the pharaohs, but it fails in representing the future of Egyptian dynasties that eventually came to an end.

I too, stared in awe at the pyramid plateau as I neared the ancient site from our bus in 1991 after our tour of Israel. Once I was standing in front of the great pyramid I could hardly believe I, a pastor from South Florida, was actually on the ground that dated back over four millennia. But getting inside of the Pyramid of Cheops was another thrill.

To gain access to the inner burial chamber [now vacant] required some doing. The ancient tunnel that ran from the exterior into the middle inner chamber was extremely difficult to navigate unless you were a small person, otherwise you were nearly doubled over through the narrow passageway. But the experience was worth it to be able to say "I crawled through the secret passageway to the center of the great Pyramid of Cheops."

When I look back on that experience, I realize that the pharaoh who built this great pyramid as a testament to his life's work and to secure his afterlife, was nowhere to be found, and the burial vault was empty. Not because of divine intervention such as Christ's resurrection that left His tomb empty, but because this burial vault's inhabitant's remains were carted off to the Cairo Museum where he resides today.

PETRA

The 1989 American adventure film, *Indiana Jones and the Last Crusade*, directed by Steven Spielberg with executive producer, George Lucas was the third installment in the Indiana Jones franchise starring Harrison Ford and others. Featured in the film was the ancient site of Petra, where the Al-Khazneh (The Treasury) stood in for the temple housing the Grail.

"It was like traveling through a 'time tunnel,'" was the response of many of the pilgrims from America that accompanied us in our 2010 exploration of Petra. We circumnavigated around the Dead Sea into Jordan and headed south to Petra. After registering our tour we walked through the "Sik" into the "land that time forgot."

Photos, drawings, maps, and documentaries do not do justice to the splendor of Petra. This ancient city—in many ways resembling a fortified sanctuary—is said to be the prophetic city where Jewish refugees during the Great Tribulation will flee to escape the tyranny of the Anti-Christ (the city's Biblical name is Bozrah, cf. Isa. 63:1; Ob. 1:3; also "Sela" the "rock").

This ancient sandstone city of Petra is an enduring monument to the primeval world of the Edomites and later the Nabataeans, established possible as early as 312 B.C.E. It is located somewhat east of the Dead Sea, in one of the most inaccessible places on earth. The rock-cut architecture and water conduit system of the city has become the monument and symbol for Jordan as well as its most-visited tourist attraction. Often called the "Rose City" due to its brilliant colored rose-colored granite and limestone cliffs, Petra was the capital of the Nabataeans and the center of their caravan trade of those merchants that passed through it to Gaza in the West as well as to other locations including the desert to the Persian Gulf.

Petra is built in a deep basin enclosed with towering rocks and watered by a perennial stream and is considered to be a fortress to this day. The city features the "Sik," [the "shaft"] a narrow, mile-long gorge between two high granite cliffs that in places is only twelve-feet-wide but descends into the area which eventually opens up into a wider valley where the first structure hewn into the sandstone cliff, Al-Khazneh can be seen. It is a royal temple-tomb cut out of the rock wall, towering 150 feet high and embellished with many finely carved columns of the Corinthian order.

Inside the city there are many buildings etched in the stone that were dwellings, forums, amphitheaters, temples, palaces, and tombs. At the "high place," north of the citadel, there is a pan-shaped altar where the animals were killed and offered for sacrifice to the Nabataean god Dushara.

Today Petra is a deteriorating monument of the Edomites and later the Nabataeans that lasted for over three centuries, but it fails in representing the culture of these two nations who eventually faded from history. Once again, man's desperate attempt to create a lasting legacy to their accomplishments gave way to the erosion of time.

ACROPOLIS OF ATHENS

In 1963, the U.S.S. Francis Marion (APA-249), an attack troop transport out of Norfolk, Virginia, dropped 1500 Marines and 300 sailors for liberty in Athens, Greece, for seven days. I was one of the sailors. Nearly all of the military visited the Acropolis, being enchanted by the rich history of the city and the ruins that symbolized a once-magnificent, but now extinct empire.

As I stood on a rocky outcropping overlooking the Aegean Sea, then turning around to see the skeletal remains of a great culture in ruins, I couldn't help but think of the Bible verses: "All men are like grass, and all their glory is like the flowers of the field; the grass withers and the flowers fall, but the word of the Lord stands forever" (I Peter 1:24-25). The glory of this empire has been reduced to a historic tourist site that had a very promising future but came to nothing as the eons passed.

During the Ottoman Empire the Parthenon was used as a garrison headquarters for the Turkish army along with a mosque that included a minaret. This was the Ottoman's way of desecrating the monument. The Erechtheum was turned into the Governor's private harem. Following the Greek War of Independence a campaign to rid the site of "unclean" influences from the Byzantine, Frankish and Ottoman periods was undertaken in an attempt to restore the monument to its original form. The Acropolis Restoration Project: The Project began in 1975 and is now near completion. The aim of the restoration was to reverse the decay of centuries of attrition, pollution, and destruction by acts of war, and misguided past restorations.[1]

OTHER ANCIENT MONUMENTS:

Many other ancient world monuments such as the Hanging Gardens of Babylon, the Stature of Zeus at Olympia, the Temple of

---

1. See "Acropolis of Athens."

Artemis at Ephesus, and the Mausoleum at Halicarnassus, the Colossus of Rhodes, and the Lighthouse of Alexandria no longer exist and accordingly have faded into history's distant memory. Vestiges of other famous monuments such as Stonehenge and the Roman Coliseum abound in our world but time has eroded their initial significance and purpose. Extant international monuments that include the Great Wall of China, the Leaning Tower of Pisa, and the Taj Mahal remain but their glory has given way to other monuments of modern times.

History attests to the folly of man's attempt to build monuments to himself that deteriorate and collapse in time. But the monuments that God builds, endure for all eternity. Question? Are the monuments you are building to self or to God?

I have thanked God often that I was born in America. Watching the news footage of our fighting forces coming home from foreign wars and the patriotism that prevailed is a testimony to the sacrifice that was made by so many. I acknowledge their service.

The freedoms that we enjoy come at a price and the foresight of our founding fathers who were willing to sacrifice all including their lives for future generations cannot be forgotten.

Fortunately we have monuments and memorials to the generous and courageous spirits that birthed the United States of America. What a journey!

CHAPTER THREE

America's Monuments

THE DECLARATION OF INDEPENDENCE

The Continental Congress adopted the famous document known as the Declaration of Independence on July 4, 1776. The original draft composed by Thomas Jefferson announced that the thirteen colonies regarded themselves as newly independent sovereign states, and no longer a part of the British Empire. Jefferson's original draft complete with changes made by John Adams and Benjamin Franklin, and Jefferson's notes of changes made by Congress, are preserved at the Library of Congress. The most famous version of the Declaration, a signed copy that is popularly regarded as the official document, is displayed at the National Archives in Washington, D. C.

The Declaration justified the independence of the United States by listing colonial grievances against King George III, and by asserting certain natural and legal rights of revolution.

Abraham Lincoln made it the centerpiece of his rhetoric (as in the Gettysburg Address of 1863), and his policies. Since then, it has become a well-known statement on human rights, particularly its second sentence:

> We hold these truths to be self-evident, that all men are created equal, *that they are endowed by their Creator* with

certain unalienable Rights, that among these are Life, Liberty, and the pursuit of Happiness. (Emphasis added)

This has been called "one of the best-known sentences in the English language, containing the most potent and consequential words in American history." The passage came to represent a moral standard to which the United States should strive. This view was notably promoted by Abraham Lincoln, who considered the Declaration to be the foundation of his political philosophy, and argued that the Declaration is a statement of principles through which the United States Government should be interpreted. It provided inspiration to numerous national declarations of independence throughout the world.[2]

This author emphasizes the statement, ". . .they are endowed by their Creator . . ." and proposes that the original architects of the Declaration were bound by their beliefs that included God in the formation of this nation. The acknowledging of God as the Creator recognizes the fundamental truths that without the Sovereign Creator, there would be no nation. The Declaration established the separation and independence from British Rule while at the same time clearly established America's dependence on God as Creator.

The founding Fathers were familiar with Scripture and revered the promises and blessings contained therein as well as the warnings and curses. It is unimaginable that these American pioneers would not refer to the Bible and entreat and invoke the Creator to superintend, lead, guide, and direct them to build a nation that would honor Him. Clearly the words found in Psalm 33 were on their minds when they penned the Declaration: "Blessed is the nations whose God is the Lord, the people he chose for his inheritance" (v. 12).

History shows that many of the leaders who founded the United States of American were people of deep faith in Jesus Christ. As an entire culture now seems intent on abandoning that faith—the very foundation that made this nation great—we offer the following words as a reminder and a challenge to live for Christ today.

2. See "Declaration of Independence."

I. . .recommend my Soul to that Almighty Being who gave it, and my body I commit to the dust, relying upon the merits of Jesus Christ for a pardon of all my sins.
—Samuel Adams [Father of the American Revolution, Signer of the Declaration of Independence]

Being a Christian. . .is a character, which I prize far above all this world has or can boast.
—Patrick Henry [Governor of Virginia]

On the mercy of my Redeemer I rely for salvation and on His merits; not on the works I have done in obedience to His precepts.
—Charles Carroll [Signer of the Declaration of Independence]

My only hope of salvation is in the infinite, transcendent love of God manifested to the world by the death of His Son upon the cross. Nothing but His blood will wash away my sins. I rely exclusively upon it. Come, Lord Jesus! Come quickly!
—Benjamin Rush [Signer of the Declaration of Independence]

Unto Him who is the author and giver of all good, I render sincere and humble thanks for His manifold and unmerited blessings, and especially for our redemption and salvation by His beloved Son. He has been pleased to bless me with excellent parents, with a virtuous wife and with worthy children. His protection has companied me through many eventful years, faithfully employed in the service of my country; His providence has not only conducted me to this tranquil situation but also given me abundant reason to be contented and thankful. Blessed be His holy name!
—John Jay [First Chief Justice of the U. S. Supreme Court]

I entreat you in the most earnest manner to believe in Jesus Christ, for there is no salvation in any other (Acts 4:12). . .[I]f you are not reconciled to God through Jesus Christ, if you are not clothed with the spotless robe of His righteousness, you must forever perish.
—John Witherspoon [Signer of the Declaration of Independence][3]

---

3. Rogers, "In God We Trust," 39.

Every signer and supporter of the Declaration, if told how America would turn their backs on their Creator and want to rid the land of every vestige of His presence—from the removal of the Ten Commandments in the courtroom to denying the praying in schools—to continuous attempts to eradicating of "In God We Trust" off our currency, they would never have believed it possible.

THE CONSTITUTION OF THE UNITED STATES

Originally comprised of seven articles, the Constitution is the supreme law of the United States of America. It delineates the nation's frame of government with its first three articles defining the doctrine of the separation of powers, whereby the federal government is divided into three branches: the legislative, consisting of the Congress; the executive consisting of the President; and the judicial, consisting of the Supreme Court and other federal courts. Articles Four, Five and Six entrench concepts of federalism, describing the rights and responsibilities of state governments and of the states in relationship to the federal government. Article Seven establishes the procedure subsequently used by the thirteen States to ratify it.

Since the Constitution was put into effect in 1789, it has been amended twenty-seven times. The first ten amendments are known collectively as the Bill of Rights. At seven articles and twenty-seven amendments, it is the shortest written constitution in force. The Constitution is interpreted, supplemented, and implemented by a large body of constitutional law. The Constitution of the United States was the first constitution of its kind, and has influenced the constitutions of other nations.[4]

The First Amendment

Few American's realize the impact that the current misinterpretation of Article One of the Constitution has had on the religious life in the United States. Article One states:

---

4. See "Constitution of the United States."

America's Monuments

> Congress shall make no law respecting an establishment of religion, or prohibiting the free exercise thereof; or abridging the freedom of speech, or of the press; or the right of the people peaceably to assemble, and to petition the Government for redress of grievances.

The definition of this First Amendment allows a person the right of free exercise whereby they can practice their religion by praying in public or in private and the right of proselytizing or the wearing of religious clothing such as yarmulkes, headscarves, or adorning a cross or a Star of David.

When the First Amendment was passed it only had two purposes. The first purpose was that there would be no established national church for the united thirteen states. To say it another way, there would be no "Church of the United States." Does the public know this?

The second purpose of the First Amendment was the very opposite from what is being made of it today. It states expressly that government should not impede or interfere with the free practice of religion. Today the separation of church and state in America is used to silence the church. When Christians speak out on issues, the hue and cry from the humanist state and media is that Christians, and all religions, are prohibited from speaking since there is a separation of church and state. The way the concept is used today is totally reversed from the original intent.[5] Does the public know this?

Yet numerous violations of the First Amendment abound when it comes to Christian values. The following are just a few:

1. 1963: The Supreme Court passes a law that removes school-sponsored prayer by forbidding the free exercise of voluntary prayer or Bible reading in public schools [Abington School District vs. Schempp]
2. 1992: The Court ruled that any officially sanctioned prayer at public school graduation ceremonies violates the Establishment Clause [Lee vs. Weisman]

---

5. Great Commission Center International, *America, Return to God*, 10–11.

3. 1998: Religious symbols [open Bible and Cross] must be removed from Ohio City Seal; declared unconstitutional [ACLU vs. Akron]
4. 1999: Homosexual activists launch a campaign to "re-educate" America's youth by introducing pro-homosexual education [textbooks and videos] to youth in elementary and kindergarten schools. "When parents expressed concern over the controversial activities of homosexual rights advocates at a high school in San Leandro, CA, they were quickly put in their place. Karl Debro, a teacher at the school and leader of the Gay-Straight Alliance, said the parents had a right to hold "their own extreme religious views." But, Debro added, "teachers have got to be free to expose their students to new ideas, so they can learn how to draw their own conclusions." This use of the public school system as a propaganda tool for the homosexual movement is merely the fulfillment of decades-old goal. . .of "encouragement and support for sex education courses, prepared and taught by gay women and men, presenting homosexuality as a valid, healthy preference and lifestyle as a viable alternative to heterosexuality." GLSEN activist and New York kindergarten teacher Jaki Williams said starting in kindergarten is a must, since children at that age are still developing their values. Even at that age, she said, "the saturation process needs to begin."

Williams, in fact, is a model teacher when it comes to this "saturation" process. She regularly initiates conversations with her children by reading such controversial books as Heather Has Two Mommies, Daddy's Roommate, and One Dad, Two Dads, Brown Dads, Blue Dads. She also hosts a view of the video, Both of My Moms' Names Are Judy: Children of Lesbians and Gays Speak Out. The intent of Both of My Mom's, is to combat "homophobia" in schools. . .Terms like "homophobia" and "prejudice" are readily thrown around the classroom, often linked with words like "hate" and "mean-spirited."

Anyone wanting to view a transformed world as homosexual activists see it need look no further than Provincetown, MA. Their education officials voted to require schools to

present a positive image of homosexuality beginning in preschool. The board also called for hiring preferences for homosexuals within the school system.[6]
5. 2000: Supreme Court rules that school prayer [at sporting events, etc.] is unconstitutional [Santa Fe Independent School District vs. Doe].
6. 2003: U.S. Circuit Court of Appeals (Alabama) denies Supreme Court Justice Moore's appeal to display the Ten Commandments in his Alabama Judicial building
7. 2008: St. Louis, MO. The South Iron Elementary School in Annapolis, MO, appealed a decision of federal Judge Catherine Perry, who issued a preliminary injunction barring the school from distributing Bibles. The lawsuit, filed by the ACLU centered on the Gideons distributing Bibles to fifth graders [Lonney Roark vs. South Iron School District].
8. 2013: A San Diego judge ruled that a war memorial located on Mt. Soledad must be dismantled because it has been found to violate a constitutional ban on government endorsement of religion. The defendant in this case was former Defense Secretary Chuck Hagel.

Purpose Of The First Amendment

The Mayflower Compact, written by the Pilgrims when first arriving on America's shores, explained that their purpose was to glorify God and propagate the Gospel of Jesus Christ. "I believe God put a hedge around this country at that time. America's first line of defense has not been the military, but God Himself. But we have politely told God to take His hedge and go back to Heaven because we can handle things ourselves."[7]

Thomas E. Woods makes it clear: When federal courts strike down religious expression in the states, they are willfully perverting

---

6. See "AFA Produces Video."
7. Rogers, "In God We Trust," 40.

the policy of what the Framers of the First Amendment intended: complete federal nonintervention in religious issues.[8]

This is not what the original Founding Fathers had in mind when they penned the Constitution since they promoted the national application of the First Amendment by allowing the establishing of religious monuments in houses of worship. They believed that the public interest was served by the promotion of religion.

THE CHRISTIAN CHURCH AS A MONUMENT IN AMERICA

When you go to church this Sunday, remember, it is a monument of light in a world presently overtaken by darkness. This must change in order for the church to survive.

As early as 1610 the Christian Church in America has been a monument to God's providence, protection, and guidance that has been the driving force that led to her greatness among the nations of the world. As a Christian nation, America has been blessed economically, militarily, technologically, and numerically under the Watchful Eye of the Creator according to his promise in Psalm 33:12: "Blessed is the nation whose God is the LORD, the people he chose for his inheritance."

In many ways there is a meaningful parallelism when we compare America with the Christian churches here in America. In both cases, they have endured through the ages despite the many wars, political differences, economic upheavals, as well as spiritual, doctrinal, and ethical challenges. The casual eye would have to admit that both America and the Christian churches in America have lasted throughout the eons of time because the Lord has been watching over them.

However, the Christian Church and its basis of authority, the Bible, has been targeted by every imaginable "ism" that aims for its destruction, or at the very least, to be pounded into impotence. From outside there is, Atheism, Humanism, Nihilism, Evolutionism, Materialism, Hedonism, Narcissism, and Existentialism. From

---

8. Woods, *Politically Incorrect Guide to American History*, 4.

inside, there is the Post-modernism, the Emerging church and "programism" designed to distract the corporate church away from Biblical orthodoxy in its teaching and application as well as subtly inject the spirit of compromise into the Christian lifestyle so that there is little difference between the godly and the profane. Jim Cymbala puts it this way:

> Instead of being a holy, powerful remnant that is consecrated and available to God (in the New Testament sense of those words), the world's value system has invaded the church so that there's almost no distinction between the two.[9]

The gradual deterioration of the efficacy of the Christian Church as a national monument can be seen with the wave of distractions that have overcome it whereby attendance over the years has taken on a new dimension. Again Cymbala writes:

> No attendance numbers can hide the fact that our new kind of Christianity is foreign to the Bible and grievous to the Holy Spirit. All over America, churchgoers chafe at Sunday morning service that runs an hour and ten minutes, but have no problem with three-hour football games on television.[10]

This form of distraction is tantamount to idolatry in the sanctuary and it is not a new problem that addresses the church. Consider the observation of a wise pastor:

> For much that is undertaken by the Church He [the Holy Spirit] is not necessary. The Holy Ghost is no more needed to run bazaars, social clubs, institutions, and picnics, than He is to run a circus. When the Church is run on the same lines as a circus, there may be crowds, but there is no Shekinah.[11]

Profanity too has infiltrated the church. Not the verbal kind, but the pretense of spirituality where the dazzling of strobe lights

---

9. Cymbala, *Fresh Power*, 22.
10. Cymbala, *Fresh Faith*, 93.
11. Chadwick, *Way To Pentecost*, 11, 13.

and the blaring noise of all-powerful audio systems designed to mimic rock concerts yields the resultant effect: "No ideals are kindled, no ministry impelled, no sacrifice inspired."[12] But we are being entertained.

The outcome of such a sacrilege is the loss of authority of the church as a national monument to God. The Church has vacated its voice through silence, allowing confusion and impotence to fill the void. This is exhibited by the approval of Roe vs. Wade in 1973 that is responsible for the death of over 60 million unborn children. Where was the voice of the Church in 1973? Why didn't the corporate church rise to the challenge and hold peaceful protests and strenuously object to the very notion that we as a nation would approve and ultimate finance the systematic destruction of our national heritage—our unborn children? Why wasn't there an outpouring from the corporate church to threaten to vote out the legislators who supported this bill before it went to the Supreme Court? The church apparently was too concerned with being "politically correct."

The Modern-Day Culprit: Post-Modernism

Do you know what Post-modernism is doing to our nation? It is undermining truth. The rise of Postmodernism is responsible for much of the erosion of conviction, principle, and authority of the Church today. This movement has attacked the authority of the Bible by undermining its truthfulness.

> Postmodernists reject both the Christian and modernist approach to the question of truth by means of human reason. According to postmodern theory, truth is not universal, is not objective or absolute, and cannot be determined by a commonly accepted method. Instead, postmodernists argue that truth is relative, plural, and inaccessible to universal reason. . .Doctrines, traditions, creeds, and confessions, all these are to be rejected and charged with limiting self-expression and representing

---

12. Chadwick, *Way to Pentecost*, 94.

oppressive authority. Preachers are tolerated so long as they stick to therapeutic messages of enhanced self-esteem, but are resisted whenever they inject divine authority or universal claims to truth in their sermons. Morality, along with other foundations of culture, is discarded by postmodernists as oppressive and totalitarian.[13]

Years ago, the pollster, George Barna reported that 64% of "born-again" Americans and 40% of "evangelical" Americans say there is no such thing as absolute truth. In other words, the Ten Commandments may or may not be valid; Jesus Christ isn't necessarily the only way to God and so forth.[14] So moving fast-forward to today, is it any wonder that the modern Church has lost its appetite for truth? This spirit of anorexia has left the one-time monument, the Church of Christ, in a weakened skeletal state. The one-time monument—the Church, the sentinel and paragon of truth—has in Nietzsche's parable of 1889, become irrelevant. Men and women may assert that God exists or that He does not, but it makes no difference either way.

> Christian values are in retreat in the West today, primarily, I believe, because of the church itself.
> If Christianity has failed to stem the rising tide of relativism it is because the church in many instances has lost the convincing force of the gospel message.
> —CHARLES COLSON. *KINGDOMS IN CONFLICT.*

---

13. Mohler, *He Is Not Silent: Preaching in a Postmodern World*, 117, 122.
14. Cymbala, *Fresh Faith*, 90.

CHAPTER FOUR

God's Monuments

THE UNIVERSE

Years ago we owned a two-acre piece of property on a hilltop in Delaware County, New York, just outside of a quaint town called Roxbury. After clearing part of the land of rocks and trees, we secured a small section to place our family tent where we would camp out for days at a time as a refuge from our daily routine back on Long Island where we lived.

One Friday night we started out after working hours and travelled through Long Island into New York City onto the New York Thruway and up to our property. We arrived at 2 A.M. in the morning at our site as our three children slept comfortably in the back of our station wagon. What followed took my breath away.

Once I turned off the car's headlights, we were overwhelmed by the blackness—we were away from any light pollution from nearby cities; there were no streetlights or traffic lights—only blackness, except overhead. I have never seen as many stars as I saw that early morning. The crisp air and lack of extraneous light gave us a clear view of the majesty of the star canopy that envelops our world.

Astronomers tell us that there are billions of stars in our Milky Way Galaxy and there are billions of galaxies in our universe, well, that early morning—we saw millions of stars that seemed so close we could reach out and touch them. I could only exclaim, "GO GOD!"

The event made me think of Abraham when the LORD God made a covenant with him: "He took him outside and said, 'Look up at the heavens and count the stars—if indeed you can count them.' Then he said to him, 'So shall your offspring be.' Abram believed the LORD, and he credited it to him as righteousness" (Genesis 15:5–6). Just imagine the view Abraham was given by God to illustrate the multitudes that would come from his ancestry. I believe Abraham slept well that night knowing that the God of the universe gave him a special viewing of His glory and majesty that we too can see today [to a limited extent] on a clear night. Please notice as you read God's Monuments that man has failed to replace, remove, alter, or corrupt His everlasting memorials.

The doctrine of General Revelation teaches that God has manifested Himself in the universe as a monument and testimony of his divine sovereignty to the nations and the world. Scriptures such as Psalm 19:1 reads: "The heavens declare the glory of God; the skies proclaim the work of his hands." This general revelation is determinately pointed to show God's majesty in his creation so that mortal man cannot deny his existence as the One that holds all things together (cf. Psalm 97:6; 98:2). Further, Paul's writing in Romans asserts that His glory is shown throughout the universe so that men ". . .are without excuse" (1:20). Not sure? Go to the Internet and type in "Pillars of Creation," M16 in Serpens in the Eagle Nebula and behold the amazing photo captured by the Hubble Telescope, then ask yourself this question: "How can one believe there is no God? Could this have just come about by random chance?"

General revelation is the self-disclosure of God to all rational beings, a revelation that comes through the natural creation and through the makeup of the human creature. All knowledge of God comes by way of revelation. The knowledge of God is revealed knowledge since it is God who gives it. Special Revelation is God's manifestation of himself to humankind in such a way that men and women can know and have fellowship with him. Special Revelation is available to specific people at specific times in specific places (cf. Matt 11:25–27; 16:17; Luke 10:21–22; John 15:15; 1 Corinthians 2:10, etc.). Jesus Christ is the central figure of divine revelation and the focus of the Christian faith.[15]

God's revelation of His creation of the universe comes to us from varied sources. There is Biblical Scripture wherein God reveals, instructs, and guides through the written word the need for response in faith of His plan of redemption. There is Jesus Christ as the promised Messiah (cf. Gen 3:15; 49:10; Psalm 2; 22, Isa 7:14; 9:6; 53; Micah 5:2; Zech 9:9; 12:10, etc.) who proclaimed that He is the way to God wherein He said: "I am the way and the truth and the life. No one comes to the Father except through me" (John 14:6). Then there is the monument of the Christian Believer who testifies by a forgiven and changed life that the work of the Holy Spirit to transform a person is real.

It was Thomas Carlyle, the Scottish philosopher, who said, "The universe is but one vast symbol of God." Although he questioned many of the doctrines of the Bible, he continued to believe in God. Ironically, he too, admitted that the universe represented the monument to God's existence. It was Eli Stanley Jones, the 20th-century Methodist missionary that looked up into the night sky and saw the overpowering star umbrella above him and said, "The universe does not make sense without God."

While these learned men testified of the universe being a monument to God, it was Dr. Robert Coleman of Trinity Evangelical Divinity School that put it all together when he observed in my hearing: "Everything in the physical world [and heaven] is designed to teach us spiritual reality." Once a person recognizes the spiritual dimension of life, they are compelled to look beyond themselves to a greater dimension—the world of the Creator. This inevitably leads us to question the origins of the universe and Who put it all together.

---

15. Akin, *Theology for the Church*, 118–19, 123.

THE MILKY WAY GALAXY: GOD'S MONUMENT TO HIMSELF

It's too bad that Creation is not taught in public schools today because it is so much more interesting than the theory of Evolution.

Creation scientists agree with the Bible that the universe is the unparalleled and unquestioned testimony to God and continues to broadcast His presence night and day as declared in Psalm 19. It is fitting that some documentation be presented:

Examples Of God's Memorials In Our Galaxy

1. Our Sun Is Perfectly Located Within Our Galaxy

   The spiral-shaped galaxy in which the earth is located is called the Milky Way. The spiraling arms and center of this galaxy contain many stars set close together giving off its characteristic brightness. Other galaxies—older, smaller, elliptical, and irregular—are missing the proper amounts of elements necessary to maintain the right balance of stars and planets required to support life. Some stars explode into supernovas, causing deadly radiation to flow though nearby stars and planets.

   The center and arms of galaxies are flooded with high amounts of radiation. Most stars are located in places with too much harmful energy for life. Moreover, at that location we could not observe farther than a few light years into the rest of the universe, because the nearby stars would completely block our view.

   Our solar system is located about two-thirds of the way out toward the edge of the Milky Way where we are least likely to suffer collisions with other stars. Most of the stars in our galaxy are within the larger spiral arms or in the center. Because there are fewer stars near us, there is a low amount of radiation surrounding our solar system. And we can observe the rest of the universe and our own galaxy much better.

2. Our Planet Is Perfectly Located Within Our Solar System
    Our solar system also contains thousands of asteroids and meteoroids. These sometimes collide with planets. Jupiter keeps many large rocks from hitting each other by attracting them with its strong gravity.
    The earth's huge moon also protects us from many of the rocks that cross our planet's path. The craters across the moon's surface demonstrate the number of times something has collided with the moon instead of the earth. The moon's South Pole Aitken basin is the largest known crater in our solar system. It is 8 miles deep and 1500 miles across. The earth's moon is unusually large. In addition, our huge moon is a stabilizing anchor for our planet. Our moon prevents our planet from tilting too far from the attraction of the sun or Jupiter. We are protected by how our solar system was created.

3. Our Planet Was Created For Life
    A smaller planet, like Mars, would be unable to hold our atmosphere, which protects us from meteoroids and keeps the temperature within the range needed for life. A larger planet like Neptune would trap too much atmosphere. The pressure and temperature would greatly increase. A stronger gravity from the increased size would also trap harmful gases in the atmosphere. Earth has a strong magnetic field. This protects us from harmful radiation from the sun.[16]

These three examples describe the complexity of the universe and the uniqueness of planet earth among the innumerable bodies in our galaxy. This is yet another monument to the Creator and His concern for humanity where He declares that human life is restricted to Earth: "The highest heavens belong to the LORD, but the earth he has given to man" (Psalm 115:16).

---

16. Morris, *Exploring the Evidence for Creation*, 64–65.

GOD'S MONUMENTS

JESUS CHRIST: THE MONUMENT OF GOD'S GRACE

The Universe beckons us to acknowledge the existence of God, while Jesus Christ and His salvation beckons us to come to him to be saved. The person of Christ and His Cross is God's monument to humanity as the only way to God.

Malcolm Muggeridge (1903–1990), the English journalist and author came to the Lord after years of living totally away from God. He writes of Christ and His impact on humanity:

> I look back on my own fellow countrymen ruling over a quarter of the world, the great majority of them convinced, in the words of what is still a favorite song, that 'God who's made the mighty would make them mightier yet.' I've heard a crazed, cracked Austrian announce to the world the establishment of a German Reich that would last a thousand years; an Italian clown announce that he would restart the calendar to begin his own ascension to power. I've heard a murderous Georgian brigand in the Kremlin acclaimed by the intellectual elite of the world as a wiser than Solomon, more humane than Marcus Aurelius, more enlightened than Ashoka. I've seen America wealthier and in terms of weaponry, more powerful than the rest of the world put together, so that had the American people desired, they could have outdone an Alexander or a Julius Caesar in the range and scale of their conquests.
>
> All in one lifetime. All in one lifetime. All gone with the wind. England part of a tiny island off the coast of Europe, threatened with dismemberment and even bankruptcy. Hitler and Mussolini dead, remembered only in infamy. Stalin a forbidden name in the regime he helped found and dominate for some three decades. America haunted by fears of running out of the precious fluids that keep her motorways roaring, and the smog settling with troubled memories of a disastrous campaign in Vietnam, and the victories of the Don Quixotes of the media as they charged the windmills of Watergate.
>
> All in one lifetime, all gone. Gone with the wind.

Monuments

> Behind the debris of these self-styled, sullen supermen and imperial diplomatists, there stands the gigantic figure of one person, because of whom, by whom, in whom, and through whom alone mankind might still have hope. The person of Jesus Christ.

Muggeridge's testimony contrasts the person of Christ and His message of peace with God against other infamous person's that have sought to dominate the world through force. Their legacy is one of war, violence, aggression, and oppression while Christ's message is one of finding satisfaction and joy in life independent of those qualities that rob humanity of life. Jesus summed up his mission when he said, "The thief comes only to steal and kill and destroy; I have come that they may have life, and have it to the full." (John 10:10 NIV)

Surrendering over our lives to Christ brings joy; surrendering over our lives to the world's system brings only destruction. The proof of this is the visible monuments to destruction that surround us today.

THE CROSS: THE INSTRUMENT OF GOD'S GRACE

When you look at a crucifix what does is conjure up in your mind? Do you see two pieces of wood fastened together as a relic of your religion or do you see what the cross represents? Some crucifixes have an image of a man hanging on it that embodies Jesus. Can you imagine the God of the universe—our Creator—being nailed to these two pieces of wood as a divine act to solve the problem of sin? Perhaps we need to look deeper at the significance of the Cross-, the instrument of death that turned out to be the instrument of God's Grace.

This instrument of death—the Cross—has become the symbol of life for the Christian. This Roman form of execution demanded that criminals be nailed to two pieces of heavy wood fastened in the shape of a "T" [Note: referred to as a "tree"]. The Persians first practiced this brutal death penalty where the chronicler Herodotus claimed that Darius crucified 3,000 inhabitants of Babylon by crucifixion. The practice spread to the Assyrians, Germans, Celts, Britons, and it is believed that the Greeks and Macedonians learned the practice from the Persians. It was Constantine the Great, the first Christian Emperor, which abolished the practice of crucifixion. Crucifixion was prophesied thousands of years before its use where we find in the Bible: "If a man guilty of a capital offense is put to death and his body is hung on a tree, you must not leave his body on the tree overnight. Be sure to bury him that same day, because anyone who is hung on a tree is under God's curse. You must not desecrate the land the LORD your God is giving you as an inheritance" (Deut 21:22–23; cf. Gal 3:13).

Yet, throughout the ages this glorious Cross has become the symbol of victory over death by the One who hung on it and vanquished death, Jesus Christ. This celebrated Cross stands today as a monument for the Church of not only Christ's victory over death, but a reminder for the Christian of the future deliverances from the finality of death. There is no memorial to God's grace greater than the Cross of Christ.

THE GRAVE

Man inherently fears death and the grave—its part of our nature. Horror movies abound with scenes of dark, dreary nights with wolves howling in the background as the camera slowly pans the cemetery, lap-dissolving burial vaults, crypts, tombstones and mausoleums, and then finally resting on two men digging at a recently dug gravesite to exhume the body to use the human parts in some diabolical plot to raise a person from the dead—thus we have a monster called Frankenstein.

But this is "Hollywood's" version of the grave, not the Bible's version. The apostle Paul gives us the Bible's version: ". . .Death is swallowed up in victory. O death, where is thy sting? Grave, where is thy victory? But thanks be to God, who giveth us the victory through our Lord Jesus Christ" (1 Cor 15:54–57). This means that only God in Christ can perform the raising of the dead from the grave. The grave had no power over Christ, and as an eternal

Monuments

monument to His resurrection; it has no power over the Christian either.

I am one of the many pilgrims who have traveled to the Holy Land to a hillside grave known as The Garden Tomb. The entrance to the Garden Tomb has an inclined ramp with a deep rut carved into it for the stone that would be rolled and placed over the mouth of the tomb to seal it. That stone is no longer there, but the resting place where Christ was laid is clearly visible inside the tomb. Yes, it is hallowed ground, since our Savior once rested there, but we rejoice because it has been unoccupied since Resurrection Sunday, 33 A.D.

Christ's empty grave stands in great contrast to those in history claiming to bring salvation to mankind. Buddha's tomb: occupied. Mohammed's tomb: occupied. Gandhi's tomb: occupied. Simon bar Kokhba whose name meant in Aramaic "Son of a Star" and hailed as a possible messiah who established an independent Jewish state and led the Jewish revolt against Rome in 132 CE that failed, was later called "Son of Disappointment." His tomb: occupied.

In sharp distinction to the so-called saviors of the world we find Christ's tomb: Empty! Testifying to His empty tomb, an angel of the Lord said to the two women who came to see the sepulcher, "Do not be afraid, for I know that you are looking for Jesus, who was crucified. He is not here; he has risen, just as he said. Come and see the place where he lay" (Matthew 28:5-6).

To the unregenerate man, the grave is a dreadful thought that symbolizes the end of all life, with some, the possibility of a future life, of which they really know not where they will spend it—in heaven or in hell? But to the Redeemed, their future is secure in the knowledge that the grave cannot hold them for when they are ready to meet the Lord; they fall asleep and wake up in His heavenly arms.[17]

Thus, the grave represents the new resurrected life for the Christian in Christ.

---

17. The picture in Scripture of the Christian going to "sleep" at death is shown in two distinct passages in the New Testament: The raising of Lazarus [John 11:11-14] and in the death of Stephen [Acts 7:54-60].

GOD'S HOLY SPIRIT—THE DISPENSER OF GRACE

The Star Wars series made popular the phrase: "May the force be with you." When I first heard this expression I realized that this was Hollywood's version of saying, "May the Holy Spirit be with you." In the Church we say, "May the Holy Spirit, lead, guide, and direct your path." It appears to me that George Lucas borrowed the term from Christianity.

But the Holy Spirit is much more than a "force." The Holy Spirit is God and the divine dispenser of Grace!

Historically speaking, Jesus Christ rose from the dead as prophesied in both testaments, but not before He promised that the Holy Spirit would come and indwell His church after His departure. This is a true monument to the promises of God. Jesus asserted: "But the Counselor, the Holy Spirit, whom the Father will send in my name, will teach you all things and will remind you of everything I have said to you" (John 14:26). The role of the Holy Spirit according to this verse then was to teach and remind. Without the Holy Spirit opening up the mind of man to understand God's Word the Bible, we would not be able to discern the true meaning of God's plan of redemption since unredeemed man is inherently unable to comprehend spiritual things. In addition, another function of the Holy Spirit is to bring to our attention the spiritual truths of the Bible once we have committed the Word of God into our hearts. Reminding us of our God's promises to his faithful and his warnings to the disobedient that the Holy Spirit's desire for truth will prevail in the life of the Christian.

The multi-faceted function of the Holy Spirit included testifying of who Jesus Christ is as Savior and Lord (John 15:26), as well as convicting the world of guilt in regard to sin and righteousness and judgment (John 16:8). The true memorial regarding the Holy Spirit, however, is the fact that he guides the Christian into all truth, and reveals to the faithful "…what is yet to come" (John 16:13). This does not mean the Christian can predict the future, but the Christian is given a keen eye of discernment in order to determine the times in which we live. This gift enables the Christian to read current events in relationship to the Bible's forecast of the future and then to make appropriate application in his/her own field of operation. Marginally, the Christian can search out the "deep things" of God with wisdom that comes from above and make judgments that compliment God's will whereas the unbeliever or "the man without the Spirit does not accept the things that come from the Spirit of God, for they are foolishness to him, and he cannot understand them, because they are spiritually discerned" (1 Cor 2:14).

The Redeemed in Christ can always look back to the monument of the promise of the Holy Spirit when it comes to difficult decisions and when it comes to temptations that dishonor the Lord, and especially when it comes to abusing God's grace. No believer of the present Church Age need ever pray, "Take not thy Holy spirit from me" (Psalm 51:11); for Christ promised His own that the Spirit would "abide with you forever" (John 14:16; Ephesians 4:30).

Paul's diatribe in Romans 6:1–14 makes it clear that the Christian is vulnerable to abuse God's divine grace but when we walk in the Spirit and count ourselves "dead to sin," we are less apt to grieve God's Spirit but walk in newness of life.

THE BIBLE—THE RECORD OF GOD'S PLAN OF REDEMPTION

When I first became a believer on the Lord and began to study the Bible, I tried in vain to find the verse, "The road to heaven is paved with good intentions." It wasn't until I asked our pastor did I discover that this phrase does not appear in the Bible, but this expression is man's way of interpreting the plan of redemption erroneously by believing that good works will earn a person entrance into heaven. So what is the Bible's record of God's plan of redemption?

The Bible stands as the paragon of monuments among written documents since primordial times. The Bible presents us with the Creation narrative and continues with the historical record of mankind and his relationship with God and winds up with a picture of what we can expect in the future. From Genesis to Revelation, the Bible as God's Word is the instruction book of the fall and redemption of man through the saving grace of Jesus Christ. Without the

Bible as our guide in life, mankind would wander around aimlessly through the ages wondering how to communicate with the Maker of the universe. But through the Bible, mankind has been given the plan of salvation whereby we can enjoy a personal relationship with God. No other book on earth has this quality.

In addition to the Bible giving an historical account of Israel and the Church, it has stood the test of time by providing humanity with the rulebook on how to live life peaceably. Noah Webster writes:

> The moral principles and precepts contained in the scriptures ought to form the basis of all our civil constitutions and laws. . . .All the miseries and evils which men suffer, from vice, crime, ambition, injustice, oppression, slavery, and war, proceed from their despairing or neglecting the precepts contained in the Bible. —Noah Webster, founding father and leader in education.

> My problem is not with the parts of the Bible I don't understand but with those I do.
>
> —MARK TWAIN

God sees His Word as an eternal legacy to who He is and says so in Psalm 138:2, a psalm of David: "I will bow down toward your holy temple and will praise your name for your love and your faithfulness, *for you have exalted above all things your name and your word*" (Emphasis added). Clearly the Bible is elevated to a prominent place in the world, behind God's holy Name and will endure for all eternity: "The grass withers and the flowers fall, but the word of our God stands forever" (Isaiah 40:8).

Is it any wonder, then, that because of these wonderful attributes that the redeemed of the Lord look to the Bible as a "treasure chest" of helpers in time of spiritual need? That the wise man or woman seeking guidance looks to the gold mine of instructions for the future? It is no mystery that the troubled man or woman looks to the Book for answers when trials and temptations assail them.

And it is because of these reasons that Satan and his demons do everything within their authority to discredit the Bible and to distract the seeker from finding God's truths and solutions to their problems. Jim Cymbala adds, "The Bible teaches that we are always either drawing nearer to God or falling away. There is no holding pattern."[18]

One of the attributes of a "monument" is its endurance to withstand the erosion that time brings and the vicissitudes of life that assails all things subject to the laws of Entropy. But this is not so with the Word of God. Peter writes: "For all men are like grass, and all their glory is like the flowers of the field; the grass withers and the flowers fall, *but the word of the Lord stands forever*" (1 Peter 1:24–25; cf. Isaiah 40:6–8. Emphasis added). In addition to the immutability of God, His word, the Bible, is a constant in our world of change. How wonderful to put your trust in the Bible, knowing that the promises and plan of God throughout the ages has never changed.

MONUMENTAL PREACHERS

Charles Haddon Spurgeon

Known as the "Prince of Preachers," Spurgeon was a British Baptist preacher who opposed the liberal and pragmatic theological tendencies in the Church of his day. It is estimated that in his lifetime, Spurgeon preached to around 10,000,000 people as the pastor of the congregation of the New Park Street Chapel [Metropolitan Tabernacle] in London for 38 years.

Spurgeon was a prolific author of many types of works including sermons and commentaries, books on prayer and devotionals. His sermons were translated into various languages and distributed throughout the world. His oratory skills and powerful sermons held his listeners spellbound and are considered by many to be the best in Christian literature.

---

18. Cymbala, *Fresh Wind, Fresh Fire*, 164.

From the day of his salvation in January of 1850 to the day of his death in 1892, Spurgeon's gift of preaching was considered to be far above average and he is looked upon today as a pillar of expositional preaching.

Frederick Brotherton Meyer [F. B. Meyer]

Born April 8, 1847, Meyer was s contemporary English Baptist pastor and evangelist as well as a friend of the American evangelist, D. L. Moody. Known as a crusader against immorality, he preached against drunkenness and prostitution and is said to have brought about the closing of hundreds of saloons and brothels.

F. B. Meyer authored over 75 books, including Christian biographies and devotional commentaries on the Bible. Meyer stands among the greatest of British preachers of his time.

Dwight Lyman Moody

D. L. Moody was an American evangelist and publisher who founded the Moody Church and the Moody Bible Institute as well as the Moody Publishers. In 1855 Moody was converted to evangelical Christianity at a church meeting when his Sunday school teacher talked to him about how much God loved him. His conversion ignited the fire that led to his career as an evangelist known throughout the world at that time.

Among the notables that came to hear Moody, the just-elected President Lincoln visited and spoke at a Sunday school meeting on November 25, 1860, and President Grant along with some of his cabinet members attended a meeting on January 19, 1876.

Literary works published by the Moody Bible Institute have claimed that he was the greatest evangelist of the 19th century. He preached his last sermon in Kansas City, Missouri on November 16, 1899, dying in Northfield, Massachusetts on December 22, 1899 surrounded by his family.

Monuments

As an American evangelist, author, and church and Bible institute founder, Moody remains one of the greatest personal Christian monuments to American history.

William Franklin "Billy" Graham

Born November 8, 1918, and dying in 2018, the 99-year-old American evangelist is noted as one of the most famous Christian crusaders of all time. Graham was a spiritual advisor to several Presidents, being particularly close to Dwight D. Eisenhower, Lyndon Johnson, and Richard Nixon.

According to his publishing outlets, more than 3.2 million people have responded to the invitation by Billy Graham Crusades to "accept Jesus Christ as their personal Savior." As of 2008, Graham's estimated lifetime audience, including radio and television broadcasts, topped 2.2 billion. He has repeatedly been on Gallup's list of most admired men and women. He has appeared on the list 55 times since 1955, more than any other individual in the world.

Since his ministry began in 1947, Graham conducted more than 400 crusades in 185 countries and territories on six continents. On September 22, 1991 Graham held his largest event in North America on the Great Lawn of New York's Central Park. City officials estimated more than 250,000 in attendance.[19]

Graham believed that politics is secondary to the Gospel, yet he has been called many times to the White House, as in the aftermath of the September 11, 2001 Islamic terrorist attacks on America to lead a service at the Washington National Cathedral which was attended by President George W. Bush and past and present leaders.

Billy Graham's love for his Savior, Jesus Christ, was the driving force that motivated him to pursue a lifelong ministry of bringing the Gospel to the world. His legacy of that message qualifies Graham as the "Gibraltar" of evangelists in the contemporary world in which we live today.

These dedicated men of God who spread the Gospel throughout the world, stand as a memorial to God's faithfulness.

---

19. See "Billy Graham."

CHAPTER FIVE

Monuments To Israel's Preservation

When our children and grandchildren were young we did not read them fairy tails or Mother Goose fables. We took them on adventures with the heroes of the Bible and stirred their imaginations by picturing Shadrach, Meshach, and Abednego in the fiery furnace and Daniel in the lions den and David's praise when he fought with the lion and the bear and then killed the giant Goliath. There was the strength of Samson and the gentleness of Ruth as reminders of God's diversity in using men and women.

All these adventures led to a God you could trust and place your faith in. Boys love the warfare scenes and the conquests of men and women who fought the Lord's battles. Girls love the narrative of the brave Esther and God's victory over the wicked Haman.

In all of the journeys, God's presence and protection was real! By familiarizing the children with the countless times God intervened in the lives of His people, Israel, we hoped to instill in them a basis of trust and hope in a covenant-keeping God. Come now; let's share some of the monuments to Israel's preservation by God.

Abraham's Monument: The Abrahamic Covenant
Imaging yourself sitting on the edge of your bed as a little child with your father sitting next to you, telling you a bedtime story. Your eyes grow heavy and you begin to fall asleep as your father hugs you

and nestles himself close to you. Then you look up into his eyes one more time as sleep finally overtakes you.

Then, unbeknown to you, your father kneels down next to your bed and extends his arms over you, and then he lifts his head toward heaven and prays that God would protect you and provide for you. He adds in prayer that God would always remain close to you and hear your prayers as you grow to an adult, and most importantly, that God would show Himself to you with His salvation.

When you awoke, what had changed? Had your father's prayer for you been rendered null and void because you didn't hear it or remember any part of it?

But you were fast asleep!

The covenant prayer your father prayed was not with you, but with the God he prayed to and himself—you were only the recipient. Because the covenant prayer was not made with you—you cannot break it—you were asleep! This is what an unconditional covenant is about.

This is what the Abrahamic Covenant is all about.

The Abrahamic Covenant reveals the sovereign purpose of God to fulfill through Abraham His program for Israel, and to provide in Christ the Savior for all who believe. The ultimate fulfillment is made to rest upon the divine promise and the power of God rather than upon human faithfulness.

The Abrahamic Covenant described and confirmed in several passages (Genesis 12:1-3; 13:14-18; 15:1-21; 17:4-8; 22:15-24; 26:1-5; 28:10-15) between Jehovah-God and Abraham was comprised of three unconditional elements. Firstly, that God would promise that through Abraham's seed, all families of the earth would be blessed (Genesis 12:3). This reference to Abraham's Seed, Jesus Christ as Messiah, would bless all those who receive Him and be justified by faith (Romans 4:3; Galatians 3:6-9, 16, 29; cp. John 8:56-58).

Secondly, the promise of a great nation (Genesis 12:2), with its primary focus on Israel, the descendants of Jacob, that they would benefit with the everlasting possession of the land promised (Genesis 17:8).

Thirdly, that Abraham would be the father of numerous descendants (Genesis 17:16). That through Abraham, the nation of Israel and other nations would fill the earth.

There was also a "protection" clause in the Abrahamic Covenant that stated, "And I will bless them that bless thee, and curse him that curseth thee. . ." (Genesis 12:3 KJV). To the nations that honor the Jewish descendants of Abraham, they will be blessed. As history has demonstrated, any Gentile nation that has supported Israel [spiritually, politically, militarily, economically, morally, etc.], have been blessed. America, for example has always been blessed as long as they have supported Israel, whereas, those nations that have persecuted or have withdrawn their support of Israel have either disappeared off the scene of history or have been significantly diminished as a world power [i.e. Assyrian, Babylonian, Greek-Macedonian, Roman, German empires]. The judgment promised to the Arab-bloc nations for their ill treatment of Israel is yet future (cf. Zech 14:1–3, 12).[20]

The Abrahamic Covenant is the living monument of God's promises to Israel, the Gentiles, and the Church of Christ.

MOSES' MONUMENT: THE TEN COMMANDMENTS

The giving of the Law to Moses and the people of Israel on Mount Sinai was both a monument to God's standards and an "insurance policy" that would act as a testimony to God's promise to preserve the nation. If they followed his commands they would be blessed as a nation. By etching His Commandments in stone, the God of Israel purposed to guarantee to His people that they would be forever and indelibly engraved on the palms of his hands (cf. Isaiah 49:16).

The first four Commandments were between God and man. The next six Commandments were between man and man. The Ten

---

20. To the Arab-bloc nations who currently persecute Israel, God has promised that their judgment is yet future. All of the nations that hurt Israel will be crushed when Christ returns at His Second Advent [cf. Ezekiel 38–39; Zechariah 14:1–7].

Commandments instructed mankind on how to worship God and how to follow His order for living a peaceful and wholesome life that would honor him. Sinful disobedience, willful defiance, and deliberate violations of God's Commandments would bring divine consequences that would act as restraining orders for society. Two examples of present-day violations come to mind: the Seventh Commandment, You shall not commit adultery (Exodus 20:14) has become a laughingstock in our nation today. With fifty-five percent of Christian marriages ending in divorce—exceeding non-Christian statistics—is it any wonder that the remaining Commandments are viewed as being "incidental" to the non-churched when the "Christians" can't keep the Commandment themselves? Also, when a nation has sanctioned the worship of multiple pagan gods in direct violation of the First Commandment, "You shall have no other gods before me" (Exodus 20:3), is it any wonder that America is in a state of "spiritual confusion?" You can ask your neighbor if they believe in God and they will invariably reply, "Yes." But then ask them what is the name of their God? You will be surprised that few will say, "The God of the Bible, the God of Israel, who sent His Son, Jesus Christ to redeem man." Go ahead, test me on this.

Today, the Ten Commandments are viewed with contempt and mockingly called "The Ten Suggestions," by those who do not want to be told by God what to do. History has proven that when a society follows the Ten Commandments and the Law of God [the Law or Torah is the Books of Genesis, Exodus, Leviticus, Numbers, and Deuteronomy] that society runs smoothly and efficiently because they are honoring God and His Book of Instruction. The added blessing is that the God of the Bible protects any nation from their enemies when they honor him.

JOSHUA'S MONUMENTS

Crossing The Jordan

When God does something important, He asks that His people build a monument to his deliverance, His protection, and His fulfillment

Monuments To Israel's Preservation

of His promises. The Book of Joshua has several monuments worthy of consideration. The dividing of the Jordan River and Israel's crossing over it on dry ground was the beginning of Joshua's monuments to God's faithfulness. God commanded Joshua to take twelve large stones from the middle of the river they had just crossed that would be representative of the Twelve Tribes of Israel and carry them to the other side to their camp at Gilgal that would serve as a marker and monument for time immemorial of God's power over nature and to His mighty hand of liberation (Joshua 4:1-7 KJV).

Achan's Trespass As A Memorial

The penalty that Achan suffered in Joshua chapter seven as a result of hiding some of the dedicated sacred booty from the battle of Jericho was for himself and his family to be executed. Despite the fact that Achan himself hatched the blasphemous deed, his innocent family was included in the death sentence because his transgression brought Israel defeat at the battle of Ai. Achan's trespass must be dealt with in order to avoid contamination of the entire nation.

After Achan and his family's execution, Joshua ordered that a stone monument ("heap") be erected to mark the place where sinful behavior led to military defeat. It was to be a warning against that criminal act that resounded throughout Israel's history, never again to be repeated (Joshua 7:19-26).

This episode in Israel's history must serve as a grim reminder that when a family member attempts to conceal a sin that impacts on the entire family, church, or nation, the entire family, church, or nation—not just the perpetrator—suffers.

The Battle Of Ai

Representative of Israel's victory over their enemies, the Battle of Ai in Joshua chapter eight is significant as a lesson to those harboring unrepentant sin in their lives. But it also serves as a military tactics lesson that will assist the Christian in times of spiritual warfare.

Monuments

God instructed Joshua to draw out the fighting men of Ai using a ruse of the Israelite's cowardice while in fact the plan was to ambush them from behind. After they were lured from the city and completely vulnerable, Israel attacked the city and captured it. After the enemy was destroyed Joshua set up the victory monument: "So Joshua burned Ai and made it a permanent heap of ruins, a desolate place to this day. He hung the king of Ai on a tree and left him there until evening. At sunset, Joshua ordered them to take his body from the tree and throw it down at the entrance to the city gate. And then raised a large pile of rocks over it, which remains to this day" (Joshua 8:28-29). God instructed Joshua to erect a victory monument to encourage his fledgling nation that in the future he would subdue their enemies if they continued to be obedient to Him. We note some spiritual "take-away" from this important battle: The Lord gives the Christian spiritual warfare instruction by providing the believer with the weapons needed to fend off or conquer the enemy. In Ephesians chapter six we are given the Armor of God necessary to defeat the adversary:

1. The Breastplate of Righteousness (v. 14) enables us to discern right from wrong; the holy from the profane, and to make decisions that honor God during a time of conflict.
2. The Shield of Faith (v. 16) gives the Christian the ability to protect his heart, soul, and mind from the "fiery darts" of Satan and his demons. The Shield defends the believer from the constant bombardment of Satan's reminders of past failures, present temptations, and future worries.
3. The Helmet of Salvation (v. 17) guards the head [and brain] of the Christian from accepting the world's view of life. The believer is given godly wisdom and the spiritual knowledge to differentiate between God's teachings and the world's teaching in life. The Christian is given understanding when it comes to the teaching of the "isms" of the world and how to avoid them. As previously mentioned, there is Atheism, humanism, hedonism, narcissism, existentialism, nihilism, materialism, eroticism, and postmodernism, among others.

4. The Sword of the Spirit (v. 17) arms the Christian with the only defense he can count on when doing battle with evil forces. When Christ was being tempted by Satan (Matthew 4:1–11), He did not react with His divine power and turn Satan into a snail and then step on him, no; he countered each of Satan's claims with Scripture. Satan, knowing Scripture (cf. Matthew 4:6) attempted to "trick" Christ by misquoting Psalm 91:11–12, but Christ steadfastly fought him off by using the covenant passages of the Old Testament that caused him to flee from his presence. In this cameo of Satan vs. Christ, Jesus set the standard for dealing with the evil one by authenticating the Word of God as the monument that endures when facing evil forces.

The Monument At Shechem

Chapter twenty-four of Joshua is an account of Joshua gathering all the tribes together at Shechem to give them a lesson in Israel's history. He recounts their deliverance from their enemies from the time of Abraham to Moses and reminds them of their conquests in the Promised Land and informs them of his family's resolution to serve Jehovah (24:15).

The people solemnly swear to serve the Lord alone after Joshua warns them of the danger of apostasy to which the nation promises obedience, the putting away of false gods, and to follow the Lord wholeheartedly. Joshua makes a covenant with the people, writes it in a book, and then sets up a stone monument to testify of the covenant between Israel and Jehovah (24:26–27).

Israel served the Lord until Joshua and those elders who witnessed God's works of deliverance died off, and then they began to follow after the ways of the heathen, thus nullifying the contract represented by the monument. If there is anything Israel learned from experience of the patriarch's history, is that they learned nothing from their experience. The cycle of Israel's relationship with God has always been: Rebellion > Retribution > Repentance > Restoration > Repeat.

Unfortunately, this same cycle is a terrible monument that can be found in the lives of many defeated Christians. But this cycle can be broken through the power of the Holy Spirit. Test God on this.

David's Monuments

David apparently learned the importance of placing monuments at certain geographic locations in Israel from Samuel the judge who resided in the hill country of Ephraim. After Samuel interceded to the Lord on behalf of the Israelites at Mizpah and the Philistines were defeated, "Samuel took a stone and set it up between Mizpah and Shen. He named it Ebenezer, saying, 'Thus far has the LORD helped us'" (1 Samuel 7:12).

The practice of setting up monuments to commemorate victories over Israel's enemies was commonplace as we have seen, but David employed a different type of memorial other than a pile of rocks. First he used his personal experience as a monument, and then he used one of the Philistine's weapons as a memorial.

When confronting the Philistine giant Goliath, David approached him with the confidence of intended victory based on his life spent in the field with his sheep and his God. While standing before King Saul just prior to the battle, he said, "The LORD who delivered me from the paw of the lion and the paw of the bear will deliver me from the hand of this Philistine" (1 Samuel 17:37). Without military training, but with total trust in the Lord for victory, David attacked the giant. Not with military armaments, but with a simple slingshot and stones. That one stone that brought down the giant would symbolize his monument. Have you a "stone" that symbolizes a recent victory?

As he stood before the giant Goliath he said, "You come against me with sword and spear and javelin, but I come against you in the name of the LORD . . .for it is not by sword or spear that the LORD saves; for the battle is the LORD'S and he will give all of you into our hands" (1 Samuel 17:45, 47). Giving full credit to his God, David was granted a complete victory over the Philistine.

Monuments To Israel's Preservation

Later, while fleeing from Saul to the city of Nob where the high priest Ahimelech lived, he obtained the sword of Goliath, which seems to have been kept in the sanctuary wrapped in a cloth behind the ephod, as a memorial of God's victory over the might of the heathen (1 Samuel 21). To the Israelites, this sword symbolized victory. When David acquired it, he did so on the belief that he would be invincible. Thus, memorials and monuments can represent victories as well as defeats. But the most momentous memorial David was known for was his writings.

David's Psalms have been an inspiration and a wellspring of good news throughout the ages to those experiencing discouragement, oppression from without and depression from within. His words have been a memorial to those seeking deliverance from the fear of reprisals (Psalm 34:4), to those overcome with troubles (Psalm 34:6); to those contentious people looking to harm you (Psalm 35:1–4), to those who repay you evil for good (Psalm 35:12), to the senior saints who can feel forsaken (Psalm 37:25), to those seeking refuge when disaster strikes (Psalm 57:1). These verses are a small representation of David's memorials to Israel and the Believer.

CHAPTER SIX

Monuments To Sin And Conflict

SEPARATION FROM GOD AS A MONUMENT

While separation from evil can be a good thing, separation from God is never a good thing.

The first monument to sin is separation from God. The expulsion from the Garden of Eden represents the first divine edict that sin was the direct cause of man's alienation from God (cf. Genesis 3:23-24). This estrangement from God is further delineated in Isaiah's statement: "But your iniquities have separated you from your God; your sins have hidden his face from you, so that he will not hear" (Isaiah 59:2). This separation is declared to be both spiritual and physical.

Spiritually and physically speaking, unredeemed mankind is ultimately remanded to spend eternity totally separated from God in the lake of fire as described in both Testaments (cf. Daniel 12:2; Revelation 20:15). The magnitude of this penalty for sin is unimaginable to the mortal man. Mortal man measures time in millenniums, decades, years, days, hours, and in minutes, being unable to reckon with God's measurement of endlessness that is void of His presence. When contrasting human understanding of eternity, one can visualize all the grains of sands on all the beaches of the world, and then imagine that each grain is one thousand years.

Can one realize what eternity is when it goes beyond that earthly measurement?

While in the body, this separation takes the form of estrangement and unanswered prayer. Due to the nature of sin in respect to God's holiness, sinful man cannot enter into a relationship with God without the covering of blood as described in Leviticus 17:11: "For the life of a creature is in the blood, and I have given it to you to make atonement for yourselves on the altar; it is the blood that makes atonement for one's life." Simply stated, when God sees the blood of Christ that was shed on the Cross at Calvary, He answers prayer. But without Christ's blood acting as the atonement covering for one's sin, prayers go unanswered as declared in Psalms: "If I regard iniquity in my heart, the Lord will not hear me. . ."(Psalms 66:18 KJV).

Throughout the ages man has questioned why their prayers go unanswered without recognizing the nature of God in respect to His holiness. Sinful man cannot approach our holy God with their petitions without the covering of the blood of Christ. This covering or blood atonement acts as "shield of insulation" to protect sinful man from being consumed as he approaches the "furnace" of God's holiness with his or her prayer requests. Without this covering, your prayers never even get to God's ears. In fact, the prayers of non-Christians are offered to demons (1 Corinthians 10:20 NIV). This is further proof of the monuments to sin and conflict inflicted on the human race.

DEATH AS A MONUMENT

As a pastor I have personally officiated over many funerals: family members, Christian church members, and even non-Christian persons. The service for a non-Christian is altogether different than for a Christian who professed Christ as Savior since the service for the Christian is a "home-coming" while the funeral service for the non-Christian is shrouded in mystery as to where they will spend eternity. Death comes to all for all have sinned Paul declares, ". . .and in this way death came to all men. . ." (Romans 5:12).

Monuments

The second monument to sin and conflict is death. The apostle Paul asserted this truth when he said, "For the wages of sin is death, but the gift of God is eternal life in Christ Jesus our Lord" (Romans 6:23). Bob Reccord comments on this Biblical text in his book Forged By Fire: "The wages of sin is death. It may or may not lead to physical death [immediately], but at the very least it will kill a part of you that God created for His glory."[21] Since the time of man's first transgression in Eden, death has prevailed over God's creation. Every form of higher life, the human, to every form of lower life, the amoeba, has been affected. All die. Mankind would live forever if it had not been for the introduction of sin into the world. Every battlefield, hospital, and cemetery give testimony to this truth—and this testimony affirms the Romans 3:23 text that all have sinned and fallen short of God's glory.

All conflict results from sin. International, domestic, or personal conflict can be traced back to some sort of sin that was the outworking of a disagreement. World wars, racial battles, ethnic disputes, marital arguments, as well as internal conflict within the heart of man, can be attributed to sin. There is the sin of pride, greed, covetousness, prejudice, idolatry, lust, jealousy, anger, wrath, inordinate affection, self-pity, and on and on—ending with the epilog, ". . .everything that does not come from faith, is sin" (Romans 14:23). In other words, if we cannot praise God for what we are about to think or do, in all probability it is sin. The prophet Jeremiah put it this way: "The heart is deceitful above all things and beyond cure. Who can understand it?" (17:9). Thus we come to understand that sin or transgression against God is the memorial that points to man's destiny, death, and that this sin is an intrinsic part of man, imbedded in his heart from birth (cf. Psalm 51:1–5).

---

21. Reccord, *Forged By Fire*, 207.

THE MONUMENT TO SIN IN THE REGENERATE MAN

Today there is a heretical movement in Christianity to minimize the existence of sin so as "not to offend people." This unbiblical view gives the false impression that sin is "off the table" as far as God is concerned and leads to what is known as the "prosperity gospel." A well-publicized preacher stated on a national TV interview when asked, "Is that a word ("sin") you don't use?" The preacher responded, "I don't use it. I never thought about it. But I probably don't. . .so I don't go down the road of condemning."[22] This "feel good" theology will not lead the unbeliever to salvation since the Bible clearly affirms that the unredeemed must recognize their sinfulness in order to repent and be saved.

John Calvin writes: "There remains in a regenerate man a smoldering cinder of evil, from which desires continually leap forth to allure and spur him to commit sin."[23] Despite the fact that the regenerate man's sins are forgiven through the divine act of redemption through the blood of Christ, the regenerate man continues to sin because it is part of our human nature. David spoke the words of God's Spirit when he wrote: "Surely I was sinful at birth, sinful from the time my mother conceived me" (Psalm 51:5). The regenerate man is forgiven of his sin and "saved" from spending eternity in the lake of fire, but the propensity for mankind to sin is indelibly

---

22. Curtin, *Waking the Sleeping Church*, 131.

23. The doctrine of Regeneration is presented in Titus 3:5 as well as John 3:3, where it is referred to as being "Born-Again." Recognition of the true character of the flesh and the corresponding abhorrence of it is one of the plainest evidences of our regeneration. For the unregenerate man is blind to the vileness of the flesh. The fact that one has within himself the conflict between the natural man and the spiritual is the proof there is two natures present, and that one finds the "Ishmael" nature persecuting the "Isaac" nature is only to be expected. That the "Ishmael" nature appears to be getting worse only goes to prove that one now has the capacity to see its real character just as the real character of Ishmael was not revealed until Isaac was born (cf. John 10:29; Galatians 4:29).

woven into our DNA, and therefore we cannot avoid committing it while we exist on the earth.

The remedy for both the regenerate and the unregenerate man is based on one's recognition of their sinfulness and subsequent repentance and then receiving the free grace of Christ's atonement on the Cross (cf. Romans 3:24). Yes, we then inherit eternal life with Christ in glory, but the "smoldering cinder of evil" remains in us but is kept in check through the empowering of the Holy Spirit. When the regenerate man does sin, forgiveness and restoration to God begins the moment confession ends based on God's promise in I John 1:9: "If we confess our sins, he is faithful and just and will forgive us our sins and purify us from all unrighteousness."

So, even in the life of the regenerate Christian, the constant presence and temptation to sin is a perpetual memorial to its baneful existence.

Idols: Man's Monuments To Sin

The popular trend in today's society is to take a self-portrait photograph with a hand-held digital camera or camera phone and post it on a social network such as Facebook, Instagram, or Twitter. It becomes what is known as a "selfie." This "selfie" is designed to give a flattering image of the person that in turn is broadcast throughout the Internet. Egomania and narcissism has taken on the form of modern-day idol making as we fashion idols of ourselves by elevating our image above everybody else.

Webster defines an idol as "an image or representation of a god used as an object of worship." Timothy Keller elaborates on this definition: "What is an idol? It is anything more important to you than God, anything that absorbs your heart and imagination more than God, anything you seek to give you what only God can give."[24] Throughout the ages man has erected idols to worship and adore. Many unknowingly pay homage to idols innocently.

Although the origin is unknown, the popular term "knock on wood" has various meanings depending on your geographic

---

24. Keller, *Counterfeit Gods*, 133.

location and is considered to be a call to alert or wake up either a leprechaun, or a good spirit with the goal of warding off bad luck or misfortune; to seek them to work in the requester's favor. Another piece of folklore adds that in the eighteenth century United States, men used to knock on the wood stock of their muzzle-loading rifles to settle the black powder charge, ensuring the weapon would fire cleanly. Then there is another belief that the knocking on wood was to wake up one's sleeping idol so that the god the idol represented would hear and answer the petitioner's plea.

Regardless of the origin and perceived benefits, the whole concept of false idols is that they represent a "man-made" deity and history testifies that these false gods are bloodthirsty and hard to satisfy and that religious dictate has never changed from the ancient ones "with its 'priesthoods,' its totems, and rituals."[25]

Today's idols come in many forms. The Bible uses three basic metaphors to describe how people relate to the idols of their hearts. They love idols, trust idols, and obey idols.[26] The human body is loved and being "worshipped" by those seeking youthful figures, often subjecting themselves to liposuction, cosmetic surgery, Olympic-style exercise programs, and the infusion of Botox to retain their young-looking appearance. Hollywood movie stars, pop culture singers, and sport "gladiators" are looked upon as images to worship. In the financial domain, the drive to succeed in business and investments in order to live a luxurious lifestyle has blinded our society to the degree that the "almighty dollar" has overpowered natural ambition, giving way to greed. If you don't become a millionaire by age 35 you're considered to be a financial failure.

Sex has always been an idol and historically, aberrant sexual behavior has become the dominant force that ultimately brought destruction on societies. For instance, phallic symbols that were engraved above the lintels of the stone houses in Pompeii and Herculaneum are monuments to the depravity of those cities. If sex is always on one's mind, then why not adorn your home with the image that you are worshipping as a constant reminder of sensual

---

25. Keller, *Counterfeit Gods*, 7.
26. Keller, *Counterfeit Gods*, 74.

Monuments

pleasure? Excavations at these Roman cities uncovered erotic art and frescoes, and inscriptions considered to be pornographic. Even many household items had a sexual theme. Many believe that the eruption of Mount Vesuvius in A.D. 79 was brought upon these cities due to their worshipping of sex.[27]

Other Monuments To Sin And Conflict

1. The Western-Wailing Wall

The highlight of any pilgrim's journey to the Holy Land has always been the Temple Mount and the Western-Wailing Wall. The first time I visited the Wailing Wall I held my breath as I reached out and touched the massive stones that date back to antiquity. I could hardly believe that I was standing on the same mount where Solomon built the Temple to Jehovah nearly three thousand years before.

Then I surveyed the Wall and beheld the many faithful Jewish men who recited prayers while wearing their prayer shawls and placing written prayer requests in the crevices between the stones. It was their way of talking to God.

The Western Wall is located in the Old City of Jerusalem. It is a relatively small western segment of the walls surrounding the area called the Temple Mount. The Wall with its variations is mostly used in a narrow sense for the section traditionally used by Jews for prayer and also known, mainly in the past as the "Wailing Wall"; this term stemming from the Jewish practice of coming to the site to mourn and bemoan the destruction of the Second Temple by the Romans.

With the rise of the Zionist movement in the early 20th century, the wall became a source of continuous conflict

---

27. The destruction of Pompeii and Herculaneum along with the Biblical city of Sodom located near the Dead Sea are viewed as memorials to the wickedness of man's nature and the direct disobedience of God's laws [cf. Genesis 19:15–25; Leviticus 18:22–30; 20:13–16].

between the Jewish and Muslim communities, the latter being concerned that the wall was being used to further Jewish nationalistic claims to the Temple Mount and Jerusalem. Today, excavations by archeologists of the Israeli IAA [Israeli Antiquities Authority] on the Temple site have unearthed clear evidence of Jewish ownership, while the Palestinian Authority disavows any such evidence and takes definite and illegal steps to dispose and conceal any ancient artifacts that can support Israel's claim.

The original Temple Mount and adjoining walls date back to the time of Solomon, Israel's second king after David (960 B.C.E.). Destruction of the Temple came at the hands of the Babylonians under King Nebuchadnezzar in 586 B.C.E., being rebuilt after the Babylonian captivity under the decree of Cyrus the Great in 515 B.C.E., referred to as the Second Temple period.

The Temple Mount came under siege once again in A.D. 70 under the Roman general Titus and was then destroyed. In recent history, the Temple Mount, along with the entire Old City of Jerusalem, was captured from Jordan by Israel in 1967 during the Six-Day War, allowing Jews once again to pray at the holy site.

The Temple Mount has been a perpetual memorial to conflict over the centuries, and will continue to be a source of struggle, even during the Third Temple period that must come about very soon according to Christ's prophecy declared in Matthew 24:15.

2. The Civil War As A Memorial

The American Civil War between the North and the South, mostly over the issue of slavery, left 625,000 dead. States rights were entirely a matter of protection of slavery while the tariff issue was of little importance. Party politics, abolitionism, and Southern and Northern nationalism, together with expansionism and economics were other contributing factors.

The American Civil War, as it was in the time of the wars between Israel and Judah, is a monument to the elusive peace between neighboring states. This war, with its hideous death count is a continuous monument to the presence of conflict in the world—even among our own citizens.

3. The Pearl Harbor Memorial

The outrage that was expressed after the Islamic terrorist attacks on America on September 11, 2001 was second to the Japanese sneak attack on Pearl Harbor. The films Tora Tora Tora and Pearl Harbor are fine reenactments of the events that led up to and the actual bombing of Pearl Harbor on December 7, 1941 by naval aircraft forces of the empire of Japan. This premeditated attack was the point of ignition that brought the United States into the fires of World War II.

At Pearl Harbor, Hawaii, the USS Arizona Memorial is the final resting place for many of the 1,177 crewmen who lost their lives when the battleship was struck with four direct-hits from 800-kg bombs dropped by high-altitude Japanese aircraft. The last bomb penetrated her deck starboard of turret two and detonated the powder magazine. This resulted in a massive explosion that broke the ship in two forward of turret one, collapsing her forecastle decks and created such a cavity that her forward turrets and conning tower fell thirty feet into her hull.

In 1958, President Dwight D. Eisenhower, who helped achieve Allied victory in Europe during World War II, approved the creation of the Memorial with its completion in 1961. The Arizona Memorial [Pearl Harbor Memorial] has come to commemorate all military personnel killed in the Pearl Harbor attack.

The Arizona Memorial is a reminder of the ongoing presence of conflict in the world that continues unabated.

4. Yad Vashem: Israel's Holocaust Museum Memorial

Israel's Yad Vashem museum serves as a perpetual reminder of the propensity for sadism, cruelty, and brutality of man to inflict on his fellow man. The exhibits that include retrieved family photographs, original newscasts, preserved

Monuments To Sin And Conflict

documents, survivor's testimonies, Nazi propaganda films, Allied Army footage of concentration camp atrocities and genocide being explored by General Dwight Eisenhower as well as the actual Nuremberg Trials film footage, is ample documentation to refute those who deny the Holocaust. It is impossible for any normal human being to come away from the experience of this memorial without only being overcome with a flood of horror and sadness at the realization of what can happen when evil is not resisted in its embryonic stages. Question. Are we seeing this reoccurring with the fundamental Islamic movement, ISIS?

Located on the western slope of Mount Herzl on the Mount of Remembrance in Jerusalem, the complex consists of the Children's Memorial and the Hall of Remembrance, the Museum of Holocaust Art, a research institute with archives, a library, and an educational center for Holocaust Studies. Included at Yad Vashem is an honored section known as the garden of the Righteous Among the Nations dedicated to the Gentiles who chose to save their Jewish neighbors from the ongoing genocide during the Holocaust. Oskar Shindler, the Nazi who helped save over 1200 Jews from extermination portrayed in the movie by Spielberg, Shindler's List, is among them.

Yad Vashem, established in 1953, is the second most-visited Israel tourist site after the Western Wailing Wall with over one million visitors each year. This memorial preserves the memory and names of the six million victims murdered and the numerous Jewish communities destroyed during the reign of Germany's Third Reich under the Nazis.

Pointed directly at the extermination of the Jewish race, the Holocaust is a lasting memorial to the evil that exists in the world that seeks to devour God's People.

5. Vietnam Wall Memorial

When the allied powers, along with the Japanese foreign affairs minister Mamoru Shigemitsu convened on the United

States Navy battleship U.S.S. Missouri (BB-63) in Tokyo Bay on September 2, 1945 to sign the instruments of surrender, the world's media announced "Peace." This peace turned out to be only a "détente," or a "lessening of hostilities" in the world since the Korean War began only five year later in 1950. Then came the Vietnam War.

Washington, D.C. is the location of the Vietnam Veterans Memorial that honors the U.S. service members who fought and died in action [as well as those that were MIA, Missing In Action or unaccounted for] during the Vietnam War. The memorial is made up of three parts: the Three Soldiers statue, the Vietnam Woman's Memorial, and the Vietnam Veterans Memorial that is the most popular of the monument.

Historically, the Vietnam War was one of the longest and most controversial wars the United States every fought and remains a national conflict without a decisive victory. This war is another testimony of the world's inability to bring about peace.

Apparently humanity is unable to build a lasting memorial to peace. The kind of peace that only comes from God.

6. Freedom Tower Memorial

What patriotic American will ever forget the scenes of the hijacked airliners flying into the World Trade Twin Towers on September 11, 2001? While the Islamic terrorists and their supporting cohorts celebrated the security-penetrating attack as a victory over America, Americans went into shock and horror at the news footage of men and woman jumping to their deaths rather than to be burned alive in the towering infernos.

The official name for the Freedom Tower is One World Trade Center, now the tallest skyscraper in the Western Hemisphere and the fourth-tallest building in the world. With a height of 1,776 feet [deliberately marking the year when the United States Declaration of Independence was signed], the Freedom Tower was built to memorialize and replace the original World Trade Center complex destroyed by Islamic terrorists on 9/11/01 and the deaths of an estimated 2,819 innocent victims.

Monuments To Sin And Conflict

Throughout history mankind has inherently sought to protect themselves from enemies. In America, we have the greatest military in the world. Our weaponry and armed forces are unparalleled, yet we could not prevent the Islamic terrorists from penetrating our defenses and striking at the nerve center of our Defense system [the Pentagon] and financial system [Wall street] to spread terror throughout our nation.

> Man wants power. There is probably no instinct of the human heart so strong as the craving for the sovereignty of power. Might is the attribute of God most coveted by men...it is the dominant passion of the human race and the key to history. The determination to possess it is responsible for more than half the bloodshed of the world and its urge has been the dynamic of civilization in all ages.
>
> —Samuel Chadwick, *The Way To Pentecost*

Clearly the Almighty has sent a message to America: Your security is not in your military or in the almighty dollar, but will only be in Me.

MEMORIAL DAY

Today's generation needs to watch the documentary series, The World at War that chronicles the events of World War II. Maybe then today's generation will appreciate the sacrifice the gallant men and women of the armed services paid for them to enjoy the freedom they do today. But alas, few remember and few give reverence to the memory of that Great War since they were not alive to witness it. How sad it is that the death of over sixty million persons could be so easily forgotten. If there's anything we've learned from experience of past wars, it's that we've learned nothing from experience—we continue to wage war with no end in sight.

❖❖❖

Monuments

Looking at your timeworn military uniform, medals, discharge certificate or papers—or even an old photograph of you at basic training or at a faraway combat zone is a monument symbolic of your allegiance to your country's heritage. "We soldiers are like cloaks—one thinks of us only when it rains" (Maurice Saxe).

Veterans, hold your head high!

Memorial Day, the federal holiday in the United States that memorializes the men and women who died serving in America's armed forces. Previously known as Decoration Day, this holiday originally commemorated the dead killed in the American Civil War between Union and Confederate soldiers. Later this holiday was extended to include and honor all Americans who died in military service.

Americans celebrate this holiday by visiting mostly military cemeteries and gravesites and the decorating of their homes with the American Flag. Family picnics often accompany Memorial Day since it signals the beginning of summer.

MODERN ALTARS OF BAAL

Baal worship in ancient Israel brought judgment on the nation. Baal worship in America will soon bring the same results. Don't think we have "Baal" worship in America? Think again.

Baal was the common name for the god of the Phoenicians and Canaanites and also the name of their chief male god. Altars, pillars, sacred trees, and memorial-stones have been uncovered that shows that Israel (particularly in the northern kingdom under King Ahab in the 9th century B.C.E; 1 Kings 16:30–33) served and worshipped the god Baal. The worship of Baal in Canaan was bound to the economy of the land, which depends on the regularity and adequacy of the rains, unlike Egypt and Mesopotamia, which depend on irrigation. Anxiety about the rainfall was a continuing concern of the inhabitants, which gave rise to rites to ensure the coming of the rains. Thus the basis of the Baal cult was the utter dependence of life on the rains, which were regarded as Baal's bounty. In that respect, Baal can be considered a rain god.[28]

---

28. See "Baal."

Baal was the also the god of fertility and the worship of this false god included sacred prostitutes participating in the autumnal orgiastic religious ritual where they performed deviant sexual practices. Human sacrifices were also a part of this cult and were strongly condemned in the Old Testament (Jeremiah 7:31; 19:4-6).

The God of Israel spoke through Elijah condemning the worship of the god Baal, known to the Philistine city of Ekron as Baalzebub ("lord of the flies"), 2 Kings 1:1-6, rebuking them for not inquiring of Him instead of the pagan god.

In the New Testament the name had changed to Beel-zebul from the Syriac language meaning "lord of the dung," a title that the Jews applied to the devil, or Satan, the prince of demons (Mathew 12:24-27), and ultimately accused Jesus of casting out demons in his name (Mark 3:22; Luke 11:15), thereby identifying Jesus as "lord of the dung heap."

In modern times the monuments to Baal has taken a broader form and instead of Baal worship to bring the rains, the god Baal is adored in his other form of veneration—sexual worship—where legalized same-sex marriage, glorification of the homosexual lifestyle, the removal of sodomy laws, the availability of youth to acquire the "morning-after" pill [tantamount to a "instant abortion"], and the proliferation of pornography has inundated America with no end in sight. In point-of-fact, Revelation 9:20-21 predicts that aberrant sexual and cult practices will continue through the Tribulation period predicted by Christ (cf. Matthew 24:15-31) into the Trumpet Judgments (more than half-way through the seven year Tribulation period).

Blaise Pascal, the French philosopher, encapsulated this deterioration of morals in America when he made the statement: "Men never do evil so completely and cheerfully as when they do it from religious conviction."

Should we come to expect immunity from God's wrath when our society has invoked the worship of Baal today?

CHAPTER SEVEN

Personal Victory Monuments

The best monuments of all are the personal ones that are inscribed on our hearts by a God, who has enabled us to overcome and persevere under trials, resist temptations, and proclaim our victories—all to His honor and praise.

Life in general is not easy. I find you have to be determined in your desires to succeed. Discipline is a word no one seems to care for but without focus and organization our lives seem to border on chaos.

In order to honor God our lives need to make sense. People are confused today as to what is truth. Is there absolute truth? When people observe a life full of convictions and faith they are curious as to how you achieve this peace of mind and spirit. My answer is "I have victory in Jesus!"

SALVATION AS A MONUMENT

In 1974 a Jewish woman who was a believer in Yeshua ("Jesus") as her messiah led me to faith in Christ. Yes, I was raised a "Christian" but had never received Christ as my Savior. "Wouldn't you want to be sure that you're going to heaven?" she asked me at a home Bible study. I nodded and said, "Of course. Who wouldn't?" From there this saint held my hand and prayed the "sinners" prayer with me. My wife didn't think I was serious, but the Lord took me at my word.

Within two years from that date, God's hand manifested itself in my life when I realized the nature of sin and how my value system was undergoing change; how many of my goals were changing; how much of my past life was egocentric and how far away from God's heart I had traveled in my former life. From that monument in time, my life has radically transformed to which I recognize that all that is important is the Word of God and the souls of men.

MARRIAGE AS A MONUMENT

And the Lord God said, "It is not good that the man should be alone; I will make him an help meet for him" (Genesis 2:18). I look down at the ring on my finger then up at our vintage wedding portrait and pause to thank God for those monuments representative of our marriage of over fifty-six years.

Marriage can either be a monument of joy like a trophy where one celebrates their victory when they marry the right person, or it can be a memorial like a tombstone when they marry the wrong person. Choosing a mate for the wrong reasons can bring a lifetime of misery and unhappiness, and a home life totally unsuitable for raising children. The 16th Century proverb, "Marry in haste and repent at leisure" has special significance when addressing the covenant of marriage. Much attention to detail needs to be taken into account when preparing for marriage or one will quickly realize that a small investment to the marriage covenant will yield small profits while a large investment will bring huge profits and no regrets.

Whether you marry for the right or wrong reasons, when the marriage includes Christ, your lives together will bear spiritual fruit without regrets. Looking through the "photo album" of your marriage may bring sorrow and bitterness, or it may bring joy and contentment, but what really matters is what you do with the time you have left. It is never too late to turn your marriage over to God through Christ and let Him manage your affairs regardless of how messy things have become because He can salvage any and all "shipwrecked" marriages. The God of the Bible is a God who sanctified marriage from the beginning and holds His Church up as His Bride—as a model relationship and guide—to be followed by all those seeking to honor Him in life.

If you are blessed with children and later, grandchildren, they may very well be your monuments to the nurturing and admonition of the Lord. Even if they are prodigals, God's faithfulness when they return is a spiritual marker to the dedicated parents who fear the Lord.

MEDICAL MONUMENTS

Most of us have medical issues that have challenged us in the past; many have scars that tell of previous surgeries, and then there are those who are facing medical situations that bring trepidation and fear.

I look at the right side of my abdomen and see a 7-inch scar. It is a reminder of a medical monument when I was stricken with acute appendicitis and rushed to the hospital where I underwent surgery to remove my appendix. I was only ten years old, but that event at the hospital saved my life. When I was stricken with spinal meningitis, the Army released the life-saving antibiotics that saved my life. I look back and realize these cases to be memorials to God looking after me. Years later I would undergo knee surgery, then hernia surgery, then prostate surgery, then eye surgery. Yet each of these operations, while insignificant when compared to major brain, heart, or organ surgery, has left a myriad of scars and scar tissue as monuments to my medical history. They also give tribute to the healing power of God toward the human heart, body, sole, and mind. My Kathy too, has "medical monuments" that attest to God's faithfulness when she underwent breast and lung cancer surgery and later, to undergo a hysterectomy to remove a grapefruit-size tumor from her ovaries, only to be followed up with a melanoma on her thigh that yielded an 8-inch incision and many complications.

> It is doubtful that God can use a man greatly unless
> He has hurt him deeply.
>
> —A. W. Tozer

PERSONAL VICTORY MONUMENTS

In time, the discomfort of childbearing subsides when we hold the child that brought on the labor pains. In time, the scars of surgery bear testimony to the hurt or wound even though the pain has dwindled or ceased altogether. So too, as a child of God, does His Spirit bring spiritual and emotional healing to those who have trusted Him when we undergo extensive tests to determine the cause of some illness, only to be told the results were completely negative, leaving us in a quandary. Later, it is determined that we have inoperable stage-4 cancer. His healing comes when we accept our destiny to be that predestined by the Lord. This defense mechanism of acceptance includes protecting us from attacks by Satan who seeks to devour us and rob us of our joy when faced with disastrous news (cf. 1 Peter 5:8).

In many ways, Jehovah-rapha, the "God who heals," allows "medical experiences" to remind us that each event is not without meaning and that He plans to use that scar as a memorial or "badge" to His healing power and faithfulness, and to use it further to minister to others. In that way God's grace is extended and He gets the glory while we get to be a shining testimony.

AFFLICTION AS A MONUMENT

Timothy Keller makes an excellent point when he writes: "People who have never suffered in life have less empathy for others, little knowledge of their own shortcoming and limitations, no endurance in the face of hardship, and unrealistic expectations in life. As the New Testament book of Hebrews tells us (Hebrews 12:1–8), anyone God loves experiences hardship."[29] Christian, believe that God has designated your affliction to deepen your dependence on Him as well as developing your compassion for others.

Medical monuments are not the only kind of hardship that can befall us. There are many other kinds of afflictions life may throw at us that bring great sorrow, often causing us to walk away from God. Suffering at the hands of others who despitefully use us, or at the hand of misfortune, failure or disappointment. Being unjustly

---

29. Keller, *Counterfeit Gods*, 358.

accused or physically or emotionally—even sexually abused can bring terrible affliction and long lasting mental anguish.

King David of the Old Testament is a monument to those facing affliction. During his seven-year persecution and flight from Saul, David numerously called out to God in his affliction and distress and soothed the agony of his soul by writing many of the Psalms. His Psalms represent a monument to his trust in God as well as a memorial to the Christian today who follows his model.

Today many find comfort and refuge by vicariously identifying with him in the times of their distress and look to David's deliverance as a preventive measure against despair. Such is the case with Psalm 34:1-8 (NIV):

> I will extoll the LORD at all times; his praise will always be on my lips. My soul will boast in the LORD; let the afflicted hear and rejoice. Glorify the LORD with me; let us exalt his name together. I sought the LORD, and he answered me; he delivered me from all my fears. Those who look to him are radiant; their faces are never covered with shame. This poor man called, and the LORD heard him; he saved him out of all his troubles. The angel of the LORD encamps around those who hear him, and he delivers them. Taste and see that the LORD is good; blessed is the man who takes refuge in him.

David wrote this psalm when he was on the run from Saul and defected to Philistine enemy territory. In a brief period when his faith lapsed, he expresses his anxiety and frustrations yet couches them in trust in the belief that God will deliver him as he did in the past when he confronted the giant Goliath; coming at the Philistine warrior based solely on defending God's honor and his past victories.

David wrote about his disappointments and fears to his Lord, but we have his writings to encourage us when we face similar trials. God's Word is our helper in times of trouble. As Jim Cymbala writes: "God does not always take us out of difficulty; many times he takes us through it. . .God uses difficulties and trouble to reveal how deep the Word of God has gone in our heart."[30]

---

30. Cymbala, *Fresh Power*, 187, 183.

The LORD is close to the brokenhearted and saves those who are crushed in spirit (Psalm 34:18).

MY CALLING AS A MONUMENT

Pastor and author Rick Warren in his book, *The Purpose Driven Church*, states: "Wise leaders understand that people give mental and verbal assent to what they are told, but they will hold to conviction what they discover for themselves."[31] Early in my Christian life I often thought of going into full-time ministry...regularly bringing up the subject when my personal sales while in the insurance business were at an all-time low, only to have my wife, Kathy, counsel me and say, "When your doing well in the insurance business, then come and talk to me about 'your calling.'" In other words, her advise meant that a calling into ministry should not come from failure, but out of success to show God's legitimacy on that calling. That indeed came five years later when "I held to conviction what I discovered for myself..." that being my calling was now of the Lord, and not of myself.

At first this calling to full-time ministry required the resigning from employment, the selling of our home, the packing up of our three teenage children and belongings, and then leave the comfort of our New York home and relatives to relocate to South Florida. Yes, we were on our way to a new life of serving the Lord—full of anticipation to be used mightily of God in His kingdom.

But however, from this point our Christian journey became very interesting.

The ministry we were called to had some infrastructure problems that ultimately caused us to leave and become members in another Florida church where I decided to return to the insurance business and also to go to Bible college to earn a degree in Christian ministry [at this time I only had twelve humanities credits earned under the GI bill]. This would become another monument in my Christian walk with God.

---

31. Warren, *Purpose Driven Church*, 156.

Monuments

After graduating magna-cum-laude with a B.S. in Biblical Studies, I was compelled to go on to graduate school where I earned my Master's in Biblical Studies while still being full-time in the insurance business. Keeping both of these demanding positions while maintaining the family and upkeep in the home was a daunting task, but the Lord was faithful to strengthen me to completion. Then in 1997 the Lord raised up an enemy to come against our household to cause us to "dig in" and change the direction we were going. A three-year "desert experience" followed and brought with it an entirely new meaning to the phrase, "trusting in the Lord." During that "drought," the Lord provide several "watering holes" where I would serve in pulpit supply as well as a part-time Academic Dean in a local seminary where I earned my doctorate degree in Christian Counseling.

It soon became obvious to me that God was using these "monuments" as stepping-stones, not stumbling blocks, and that these monuments or blessings in disguise would become a memorial to God's faithfulness.

In the course of time this ministry meandering began to unbend when I was called to full-time pastoring. The church incorporated a multi-cultural ministry that presented many challenges but all the time the joy of the Lord was present. Another memorial that reaffirmed my conviction to ministry!

Then after six years it was time to pull up the tent stakes and move on!

The call to co-pastoring a church was the next step in our journey. While this joint leadership position at times was difficult, there were years where the Lord used my wife, Kathy, and I to bring solid teaching and preaching, along with Biblical counsel to those in the congregation.

In the sixth year of our co-pastoring, our family suffered a major disaster when our eldest son died of complications arising from heart issues. Composing ourselves to give the tribute and eulogy to our son at his funeral was the hardest thing we ever had to do. Soon after this tragedy we sold our home in South Florida and relocated to North Florida. We needed a change to help us heal and find closure.

Personal Victory Monuments

Today, I am looking at a rock that sits on my desk as I write this account of our journey. On the top it reads, "VICTORY MONUMENT" written with a blue permanent marker pen. Circling the rock are Bible verses, dates, and events that have occurred over the years. Titles such as "Free from family emergency," [This victory marked our son going to heaven], and "Free from medical concerns" [This victory marked the survival of Kathy's breast cancer surgery]. These markers serve as reminders to me when I experience periods where I fall short of my faith in the Lord. They are a source of encouragement when doubts creep into my heart and Satan attempts to rob us of our joy by suggesting that the Lord has abandoned us or that our faith is weak and we cannot be used any longer. Lies! That's what they are, but they serve a greater purpose—to prompt you to realize that for the Christian soldier, this life is not a playground but a battleground.

But praise the Lord; He is the Commander of the Hosts of heaven!

CHAPTER EIGHT

Recognizing Your Monuments

THE MONUMENT OF SALVATION

The rainbow that follows a rain shower is a beautiful image of the covenant the God of the Bible made with man after the global flood of Noah. It is a memorial to his promise that "never again shall the water become a flood to destroy all flesh" (Genesis 9:13-16). The Noahic Covenant reaffirms the promise that continues to today that the end of the world will not come by a worldwide flood.

It is this symbol along with numerous other promises that God has made to humanity, His people Israel, and to His Church that engenders trust and brings hope to those who put their faith in Him. The 3-fold promise that God made to Abraham and the Israelites along with the promise that Christ made to his Church are striking monuments that validate the entire plan of salvation and are examples of God's unconditional promises.[32]

The gift of salvation that brings with it the doctrine of eternal security cannot be minimized since it is an everlasting memorial to

---

32. The three-fold Abrahamic Covenant is located in Genesis 12:1-3; 15:1-6, 18-21. The covenant Christ made with the Church is located in Matthew 16:17-19; 1 Peter 2:4-8; 1 Cor 3:11 where upon Christ the Rock the Church will be built.

the immutability of the divine counsel of God.[33] The Christian has this monument, or corner stone, to build his or her life on since the unbreakable promise of spending all eternity in heaven with their Savior eclipses all of life's problems and should constantly renew their joy and purpose.

BUILDING ON THE MONUMENT OF SALVATION

The monument of salvation provides the foundation in which to build the Christian Life in Christ. The new Christian will experience life-changing revelations as the Holy Spirit begins to show them by sharp contrast the difference between the holy and the profane, or the lifestyle that needs to be conformed to the image of God so that they can be mightily used in the kingdom plan.

In His mercy, the Lord brings about the sanctification [or the "setting apart" to holiness] gradually (cf. Romans 12:2). We would be overwhelmed and very discouraged if the Holy Spirit were to expose our inequities all at once. The unfolding picture of this truth is found in the book of Joshua. God commanded Joshua to lead the children of Israel into the Promise Land, the land of Canaan, and systematically overpower, destroy and occupy those heathen nations that occupied the land. Over the period of three campaigns the occupying people of the Canaanites, the Hittites, the Hivites, the Perizzites, the Girgashites, the Amorites, and the Jebusites were to be conquered and displaced by the Israelites (Joshua 3:10).

This is a picture of how the Holy Spirit systematically works on our old sinful nature and shows us what areas of our life must be sanctified and come under the new headship of Christ.

Fortunately for the new Christian, the Lord is very gracious and slowly works with us to overcome those attitudes, worldly goals, and sins that grieve Him so that in time we replace them with godly attributes. For many this process of sanctification may come

---

33. The doctrine of eternal security is amply defined in Scripture. Christ defined it in John 3:36 since He alone brings eternal life, John 5:24, 14:6; 1 John 5:13, and that the Christian's salvation is secure in Christ, John 10:28. The regenerated Christian cannot lose their salvation, regardless of sin.

about in a short period of time, for others it could be a lifetime. The expediting factor is a matter of claiming Christ as Savior by faith, thus experiencing peace with God (Romans 5:1), and then proceeding to surrender to Him as Lord of your life, with the consummate experience of the peace of God (Philippians 4:7).

With Christ as the foundation the building that is erected will withstand the calamities that befall the human race, the storms of adversity, and the temptations of the flesh that follow man's sinful predisposition. When the Christian appropriates the grace of God to adversity and the power of His Spirit to temptation, they cannot fail.

In turn, these victory monuments enable the Christian to minister to others even as the Holy Spirit has ministered to us (Hebrews 6:10; 1 Peter 4:10). In this way our service is pleasing to God and a testimony to our salvation.

SPIRITUAL MILESTONES AS MONUMENTS

Leading a non-Believer to salvation in Christ is without question the greatest monument a Christian can claim for oneself, all to the glory of God. This milestone places the feet of the veteran Christian on a path that not only exhilarates them in the Lord, but also encourages the new convert to embark on their own campaign of evangelism. Although the *Four Spiritual Laws* pamphlet by Bill Bright in the hands of a Christian is a useful tool to witness to a non-Believer [as well as other evangelical tracts], the Christian's testimony is by far the most effective. Seeing a person's life change to honoring the Lord—speaks volumes to the non-Christian.

When the Spirit of God enables a new Believer to navigate, study, and understand the Bible, this too is a monument to the ongoing work of God. The task of the Spirit is to impress upon the Christian the need to stay in God's Word and to have a passion for the lost souls in the world. In addition, the Spirit invokes a change in behavior of the new Believer where their life takes on a different demeanor, one that honors the Lord when they give up their old way of life (cf. 2 Cor 5:17).

Recognizing Your Monuments

> Charles Spurgeon once said that when a jeweler shows his best diamonds, he set them against a black velvet backdrop. The contrast of the jewels against the dark velvet brings out the luster. In the same way, God does his most stunning work where things seem hopeless.
>
> —Jim Cymbala, *Fresh Wind, Fresh Fire*

Overcoming God-ordained trials and hardships while still praising and trusting in the Lord is a glaring testimony and signpost to both the corporate Church and the secular world. The brethren must acknowledge your acceptance and endurance and conclude, "If he/she can do it with all they're going through, so too can I!" This mindset serves as a template for those struggling with the trials and hardships of life; yielding them over to the Lord's safekeeping.

To the unredeemed, their response is, "How do you do it? If it was me, with everything that is going on in your life, I would just curl up in a ball in some corner and stay there, crying out, leave me alone!" This monument gives the Christian an opportunity to give their testimony and share Christ with them—something that may not have happened without the trial you're undergoing at the time.

Experience in ministry dictates that when a Christian dies, their funeral is one of the grandest milestones in the world, and their final monument. Even before death overtakes the ailing Christian, the Spirit of God brings a wonderful calmness and longing to be with their Lord in glory. God's spirit places in them a desire to be with the Lord who saved them and they begin to mentally detach themselves from the allure of the world with all of its trimmings. Yes, leaving behind their loved ones is very difficult and has with it commensurate sadness, but God's Spirit assures them that their safekeeping is in God's hands and they are no longer to be concerned with those left behind.

This is the final monument to life in Christ.

PERSONAL PRAYER MEMORIALS

Cornelius, a centurion in the Italian Regiment, was a God-fearing believing man who lived during the first century church. One day he had a vision from God and an angel appeared to him and called him by name saying, "Your prayers and gifts to the poor have come up as a memorial before God" (Acts 10:3).

Prayers recognize God. Atheists are unfamiliar with prayer, but to the Christian, prayer is a memorial and a much-needed weapon against the antagonizing forces that seek to discourage them.

A prayer journal is a constant diary of both answered and yet-to-be-answered prayers, and serves as a memorial, especially during the dark periods of the Christian life when adversity strikes. When life takes a turn for the worse, reviewing your answered prayer log brings wonderful encouragement as you remember dates and outcomes of the petitions that at one time beset us—now with joy unspeakable.

Recording our prayer requests serves as a kind of "release" as if we wrote them down and placed them "on the altar" before God, pledging not to be troubled by the dilemma until our next encounter or prayer meeting with Him.

When an emergency suddenly comes upon us, either nationally or personally, we may not have enough time to organize a prayer chain or formulate a written prayer, but only cry out, "LORD, HELP!" These too are to be memorials when the Lord delivers us from the sudden calamity and He brings relief. [Example in Appendix A].

Then Jesus told his disciples a parable to show them that they should always pray and not give up...(Luke 18:1).

GOD'S BENEFITS AS MEMORIALS

In today's corporate world group insurance benefits have become a major player when deciding on employment choices. King David was concerned with benefits as well when he penned,

> Praise the LORD, O my soul, and *forget not all his benefits*—who forgives all your sins and heals all your diseases, who redeems your life from the pit and crowns you with love and compassion, who satisfies your desires with good things so that your youth is renewed like the eagle's (Psalm 103:2–5, Emphasis added).

Throughout David's life, as expressed in this psalm, he continuously thanked God for the benefits bestowed upon him despite the treachery inflicted upon him from King Saul. He cited in his other psalms the benefit of forgiveness of sin (cf. Psalm 51:1–4, 9), the Lord's healing power (cf. Psalm 41:4), the gift of redemption (cf. Psalm 49:15), and the satisfaction of his desires (cf. Psalm 37:4). To David, God's benefits were monuments that he could look back on to give him the spiritual fortitude to go on and face life's challenges. To David, the benefits were so real and relevant that he wrote them down so that others may benefit from his experiences.

It has been said that God's benefits "are out of this world." While that is true, Christ declared that we don't have to wait 'til we get to heaven to slice into God's benefits when he said, "The thief comes only to steal and kill and destroy; I have come that they may have life, and have it to the full" (John 10:10). A "full" life is not necessarily one of continued success or the accumulation of material "stuff," but from a kingdom perspective, it is more like: The empowerment of the Holy Spirit when witnessing your faith to an unbeliever, or the empowerment of the Holy Spirit to overcome a nagging sin, or the empowerment of the Holy Spirit to bring to mind Scriptures when preaching God's Word or teaching at your Sunday School class. Then there is the empowerment of the Holy Spirit where the Believer is given special discernment to counsel a fellow Christian during a time of crisis (cf. Romans 15:14; Colossians 3:16). Other "benefits" include God's provision where He promises to provide all of your needs according to His riches in Christ Jesus (Philippians 4:19).

Remember these benefits when going through difficult times, and your petitions will turn into praises.

MONUMENTS

PRESENT AND FUTURE CROWNS AS MEMORIALS

Hannah Whitall Smith writes in her celebrated book, *The Christian's Secret of a Happy Life,* "It is altogether the way we look at things, whether we think they are crosses or not. And I am ashamed to think that any Christian should ever put on a long face and shed tears over doing a thing of Christ, which a worldly man would be only too glad to do for money." I believe her poignant statement can apply to our attitude towards earning crowns for the Lord as well. We should be willing to work for the Lord so that He can coronate us with crowns either in this life or the next, or both—not that we would receive worldly accolades—but spiritual crowns.

When Christ the Revealer of Secrets, He who is Faithful and True, returns on his white horse to bring judgment on he earth, He will be wearing many crowns (Rev 19:11–12). On that day, every eye will see Him and every tongue confess that He is Lord. But these crowns are different than the crown He bore on earth since that crown was one of thorns, a crown of suffering. Yet, it proved to be a crown of victory over sin and death.

Christians are eligible for crowns as well, both in the present as well as in the future. For those who long to please their Lord now there are crowns that are available today. But as with Christ, the crowns come at a price that many are not willing to pay (cf. 2 Tim 2:5–6).

Crowns are ornaments of triumph that often accompany rewards and serve as a memorial to the victor when they achieved mastery over their opponent and won the battle. In the Christian life the believer can earn crowns that are evidenced by their testimony and the life they exhibit. Jesus made it clear that His believers will exhibit fruit and that fruit will bear more fruit (Matthew 7:16).

> No Cross, no Crown.
>
> —Thomas Fuller, MD

Certainly a Christian wins a crown here on earth when they display the fruit of the Spirit (cf. Galatians 5:22-23). By demonstrating love, joy, and peace, etc., in the face of confrontation or adversity that in turn gives glory to God, the Christian is emboldened to work harder to grasp more of the Holy Spirit for the next encounter. By holding out from temptation of the flesh and exhibiting self-control, not only is that a tremendous testimony, but it too engenders a "try harder" mentality for the next session of temptation. These victories are crowns in this life that convert to tools that bolster and uphold the Christian when challenged or embattled.

At the heavenly Bema Seat Judgment, crowns will be bestowed on the believing Church (2 Cor 5:10). The Crown of Life is awarded to those who not only endure but overcome temptation (James 1:12). The Incorruptible Crown is awarded to those who overcome the old sinful nature and bring their body into subjection to the leading of the Holy Spirit (1 Cor 9:24-27). To those who have suffered and were persecuted for Christ's sake will receive the Crown of Glory (James 1:12; 1 Peter 5:1). The Crown of Righteousness will be awarded to those anticipating and preparing the harvest of souls for Christ's Return (2 Tim 4:8). Last, but certainly not least, is the Crown of Rejoicing that is conferred upon those soul winners who did not grow weary in well doing but continued in the fight to bring the lost to Christ (1 Thess 2:19). These crowns will serve as reminders to those monuments we built while in the natural world.

I am coming soon. Hold on to what you have, so that no one will take your crown (Rev 3:11).

SECULAR ACHIEVEMENTS AS MEMORIALS

School Achievements

I know of many men and women who married without a college or graduate degree and sacrificed and waited until their families were grown and on their own before completing a degree program. I am one of them. After my children completed their education, I felt compelled to return to college and then on to seminary to finish my degree program. This was a glorious time in my life [despite the fact that I was working full time in my secular job].

Graduating with a college degree is certainly an achievement that qualifies as a monument. Graduating with a Master's or Doctorate degree from a graduate school is an even greater monument that is represented by the diploma and the exhilarating feeling of accomplishment. After years of grueling studies, exams, and papers, and of course the consummate work, the thesis and dissertation—one deserves to celebrate and record the event in such a way as to remember it the rest of their lives. When the graduate gazes upon the diploma hanging above their desk, this is a monument to their achievement.

Military Achievements

Military decorations are also monuments. Awards for accomplishments performed in the line of duty such as The Congressional Medal of Honor, The Purple Heart, and The Distinguished Service Medal, etc. recognize the bravery, valor, and sacrifice made by those defending liberty in the United States.

Every member of the Armed Forces with an Honorable Discharge can proudly proclaim that document as a monument to their military service. These memorials stay with the veteran recipient forever as a permanent part of their service record. Many retail stores recognize veterans and offer well-deserved discounts for goods and services.

Sports And Other Achievements

Sports and academic trophies and awards are yet other memorials that contribute to the monuments that life has to offer for those who go beyond the norm. Recognition celebrations and plaques upon retirement after many years of faithful employment represent monuments for many retirees who look upon their years of work with pride and satisfaction.

Financial Monuments

The "mortgage-burning" celebration is perhaps the best kind of financial monument a homeowner can enjoy. Once the mortgage is paid off the mortgagee can look back on the years of payments and revel in the triumph.

Completing the car payments schedule and the student loans stands as a memorial to the perseverance of the payer as well as paying no interest on a revolving charge account—a monument to the discipline of the cardholder.

To those who pay cash or have reached that point of discipline in life to "do without" something in order to avoid credit—they receive the monument of extreme satisfaction!

CHAPTER NINE

The Ultimate Crowning Glory Monument

In the parable of the Talents, Christ explains that the worker who put his money to work and earned a profit was told, "Well done, good and faithful servant! You have been faithful with a few things; I will put you in charge of many things. Come and share your master's happiness" (Matthew 25:21-24). To the worker who received one talent and complained, "I knew that you are a hard man, harvesting where you have not sown and gathered where you have not scattered seed. So I was afraid and went out and hid your talent in the ground. See, here is what belongs to you," Christ rebuked him then accused him of being a wicked, lazy servant who neglected to use the investment to earn interest.

    This parable can be applied to those to whom God has given the special grace that leads to salvation, the grace that enables us to overcome sin's temptation, as well as the struggles and failures in life. The parable is also a reminder that "interest" will be paid to those who appropriate God's grace.

    This parable also can be applied to those Christians whom God has given the power of the Holy Spirit to testify boldly of Christ's forgiveness and stand fast on God's Word the Bible when faced with secular reasoning that easily leads to compromise and the discrediting of the Holy Scriptures.

The Ultimate Crowning Glory Monument

To them belongs the Crowning Glory, the Ultimate Monument: "Well done, good and faithful servant!"

EFFECTIVE MEMORIALS

In order to achieve the spiritual heights we long for, it is necessary for us to recognize the memorials God has brought into our lives—memorials we may have forgotten as we advance in age or are confounded by undesirable circumstances in our world.

In Matthew sixteen Christ rebukes the Pharisees who did not understand Him in their spiritual blindness when they came to test Him by requiring a sign from heaven to legitimize His claim to deity. He responded, "A wicked and adulterous generation seeks after a sign, and no sign shall be given to it except the sign of the prophet Jonah" (Matthew 16:4). Christ referred to the sign of His resurrection that would occur after he spent three days in the earth following His death on the cross. He would not patronize those who sought to undermine His purpose or plan of redemption. In the next verse (v. 5), the text adds that His disciples followed Him yet, "...they had forgotten to take bread."

Jesus then challenges His disciples to check their spiritual progress by explaining, "Take heed and beware of the leaven of the Pharisees and the Sadducees (Matthew 16:6). The next text states that, "And they reasoned among themselves, saying, 'It is because we have taken no bread'" (16:7).

Christ then points out that as his disciples, they did not pass the quiz. He questions their immature faith and lack of understanding spiritual matters and says, "*Do you not yet understand, or remember the five loaves of the five thousand and how many baskets you took up? Nor the seven loaves of the four thousand and how many large baskets you took up? How is it you do not understand that I did not speak to you concerning bread?—but to beware of the leaven of the Pharisees and Sadducees*" (16:9-11 Emphasis added). Christ was reminding them of their need to remember these miracles and spiritual explanations He gave them as memorials and monuments in their lives if they are to grow in grace and knowledge of the Lord and be effective in their future ministry. The section of text under considerations ends with "Then they understood that He did not tell them to beware of the leaven of bread, but of the doctrine of the Pharisees and Sadducees" (v. 12). To Christ, memorials and monuments are important in order for us to grow in grace and remember the knowledge of who He is, and to be effective in our ministry.

REFLECTIONS

Can we agree on the truth of how good God has been to us? When we reflect on the goodness of God demonstrated toward us, instead of the consequences due us from wrongdoing, we must settle the question, how do we respond?

Reflecting on His goodness should be the outworking of the awareness of the monuments we have established in our lives. This must compel us to look back on His goodness displayed by His protection, provision, and most importantly, His presence in our lives.

APPENDIX A

PRAYER OF NATIONAL REPENTANCE

Heavenly Father, we come before you today and ask Your forgiveness and to seek your direction and guidance. We know Your Word says, "Woe to those who call evil good," but that is exactly what we have done. We have lost our spiritual equilibrium and reversed our values. We confess that:

We have *ridiculed the absolute truth of Your Word* and called it *Pluralism*
We have *worshipped other gods* and called it *multiculturalism*
We have *endorsed perversion* and called it *alternative lifestyle*
We have *exploited the poor* and called it the *lottery*
We have *rewarded laziness* and called it *welfare*
We have *killed our unborn* and called it *choice*
We have *shot abortionists* and called it *justifiable*
We have *neglected to discipline our children* and called it *building self-esteem*
We have *abused power* and called it *politics*
We have *coveted our neighbor's possessions* and called it *ambition*
We have *polluted the air with profanity and pornography* and called it *freedom of expression*
We have *ridiculed the time-honored values of our forefathers* and called it *enlightenment*

PRAYER OF NATIONAL REPENTANCE

"Search us, Oh, God, and know our hearts today; cleanse us from every sin and set us free. Guide and bless these men and women who have been sent; to direct us to the center of Your will and to openly ask these things in the name of Your Son, the living Savior, Jesus Christ, Amen."

—Rev. Joe Wright
[at the session of the Kansas Senate, January, 1996]

Bibliography

"Acropolis of Athens." https://en.wikipedia.org/wiki/Acropolis_of_Athens.
"AFA Produces Video to Counter Homosexual Propaganda Film." *American Family Association Journal*, April 1999. https://afajournal.org/past-issues/1999/april/afa-produces-video-to-counter-homosexual-propaganda-film/.
Akin, Daniel L., ed. *A Theology for the Church*. Nashville: B& H Academic, 2007.
"Baal." https://en.wikipedia.org/wiki/Baal.
"Billy Graham." https://en.wikipedia.org/wiki/Billy_Graham.
Chadwick, Samuel. *The Way To Pentecost*. Berne, IN: Light and Hope, 1937.
"The Constitution of the United States." https://en.wikipedia.org/wiki/Constitution_of_the_United_States.
Curtin, Ralph D. *Waking the Sleeping Church*. Savage, MN: Lighthouse, 2009.
Cymbala, Jim. *Fresh Faith*. Grand Rapids: Zondervan, 1999.
———. *Fresh Power*. Grand Rapids: Zondervan, 2001.
———. *Fresh Wind, Fresh Fire*. Grand Rapids: Zondervan, 1997.
"Declaration of Independence." https://en.wikipedia.org/wiki/Declaration_of_independence.
Great Commission Center International. *America, Return to God*. Sunnyvale, CA: 2006.
Keller, Timothy. *Counterfeit Gods: The Empty Promises of Money, Sex, and Power, and the Only Hope that Matters*. New York: Dutton, 2009.
Mohler, R. Albert, Jr. *He Is Not Silent: Preaching in a Postmodern World*. Chicago: Moody, 2008.
Morris, Henry M., III. *Exploring the Evidence for Creation*. Dallas: Institute for Creation Research, 2009.
Reccord, Robert E. *Forged By Fire: How God Shapes Those He Loves*. Nashville: Broadman & Holman, 2000.
Rogers, Adrian. "In God We Trust." *Decision Magazine*, July/August 2014.
Warren, Rick. *The Purpose Driven Church: Growth without Compromising Your Message and Mission*. Grand Rapids: Zondervan, 1995.
Woods, Thomas E., Jr. *The Politically Incorrect Guide to American History*. Washington, DC: Regnery, 2004.

www.ingramcontent.com/pod-product-compliance
Lightning Source LLC
Chambersburg PA
CBHW071200090426
42736CB00012B/2398